JOSH PENNELL

'The Family Finance Guy'

What Parents Want

Achieve financial freedom, life balance and family happiness

R^ethink

Disclaimer

*To my dearest JP, Little Princess, Toots, Ollie and
Raffi Boy*

Thank you for all the love and laughs

Create a life that brings you joy and happiness

Contents

Introduction

As busy parents, we have so much on our plate. I like to call us jugglers. We are constantly juggling different demands and responsibilities: a career or business to run; kids to raise and taxi around; and a relationship to maintain. That's before we find time to stay fit and healthy, socialise, be there for friends and family and chip in at the local sports club, school committee or charity. Oh, and sleep. We'd better make some time to sleep.

Does all this resonate with you?

Competing demands can lead to a life that's a hot mess of frantic survival. This book will replace that mess with a clear, calm and enjoyable flow. It will help you achieve greater wealth and financial freedom, a better lifestyle and all the happiness and success you truly desire for yourself and your family.

As a dad to four kids aged five, eight, twelve and thirteen and the owner of a successful business, I truly understand the 'juggler' title. My partner also works and our kids have a lot going on in their lives, so our household is smack bang in the middle of the 'craziness' phase of family life. While busy, it is also a well-balanced, happy life and we enjoy the things we value most. I am extremely grateful to have an amazing partner and four healthy, beautiful kids.

If I go back about five years, things were different. My partner and I didn't even know each other. We were living in two separate families. I had a lot of amazing things in my life: a healthy three-year-old son who I had a great bond with; a daughter on the way; a successful business as well as an exciting start-up company that had signed customers in fourteen countries. I had just purchased and moved to a home 100 metres from the beach in one of the most popular holiday destinations in Australia with stunning ocean, mountain and lake views and sunsets to die for from the deck overlooking the pool. I could walk barefoot along the ocean front and down into a beautiful bush track to an amazing surf beach, spotting numerous wallabies, echidnas, dolphins and blue-tongued lizards along the way. As I'm a nature, outdoors and ocean lover, it truly was the definition of my dream home.

Despite all these great things in my life, at the time, my marriage wasn't going so well and ultimately ended in separation and divorce. That meant I had to move out of my beautiful home and led to the failure of my start-up company as I needed to focus on my kids and existing business, so while there were a lot of positives in life, not all areas were going well or in balance.

No one gets married planning to get divorced and it's a terribly stressful and hard event for anyone, but sometimes things just don't work out. That can happen in all areas of life, not just in relationships. But often great things come from challenging times. It's where we can learn, grow and evolve to create better outcomes in the future. Having now brought my kids together with an amazing new partner and her two kids, I've been through the big life event of creating a happy blended family. I know the experiences I've had helped me learn and grow, and by reading, trying, testing and opening my mind up to new things, I have found some amazingly helpful tools that I believe are valuable to other parents and families across numerous facets of their lives.

The knowledge I gained from this experience makes me the perfect person to teach others. Rather than going through all the challenges I did, you can implement my learnings in your life. Throughout this book, I will pass on the lessons that can only come with hindsight and life experience. I have evolved and developed these into a clear set of easy-to-follow methods that you and your family can employ to help you avoid mistakes and achieve better balance, outcomes and results across all areas of your life.

In addition to my family-related experiences, I started investing at the age of fifteen and since then have invested across a wide range of public global companies, properties and privately owned businesses. I have been a wealth management and investment advisor for eighteen years and have advised clients with investment portfolios as large as $40 million and incomes of many millions of dollars per year. Just as importantly, I have helped hundreds of families who don't have that kind of money to achieve financial and lifestyle success.

Via my many client interactions over eighteen years, I have learned that money alone does not make people or families happy. It's achieving what I call Fulfilled Family Wealth – the beautiful intersection of hitting financial, lifestyle and family goals simultaneously – that can create a dream life.

Life as a busy parent can be so complex, it may leave people feeling confused, exhausted, overwhelmed and unfulfilled. Even if we have a great income or a lot of money, we still don't feel like it's all working 'right'. The potential risks and costs of continuing along this path for too long are huge – my own failures pay testament to the toll it can take. It is all too easy for weeks to become months and years as we go through life in a blur of 'doing', but not 'achieving' what we really desire.

Having seen this happen in my own and in many clients' lives, I have learned to recognise some clear trends. I know what pins people down to a point of security and safety, as well as the forces that are making them unbalanced, and this led me to create the Parental Balance Model. This will help you better visualise the most common pressures and demands across a range of areas that are all intertwined. Having this model in your life will allow you to understand these pressures and balance them out so you can calmly walk to optimum results. In this book, I will explain how to follow the most efficient path to the things you want.

At its core, this book is about money. If you follow the advice within its pages, you will achieve financial freedom and security and become wealthy, but I promise not to bore you to death with endless numbers or financial jargon. Its scope is much broader than just teaching you how to gain a big pile of cash. This book will make you both *rich* and *enriched*.

I will help you move from confusion to clarity, guiding you to create a succinct vision of what you really want. Then my set of clear methods and models will provide a simple and efficient process for obtaining it, leaving you more relaxed, less stressed and with plenty of quality time for yourself and your family. Your finances will become well structured and understandable, so you can have more money and energy going towards the things that truly matter to you. The wealth machine will give you a repeatable process for growing your wealth and improving your life so your money will work for you, instead of you working for money.

Furthermore, you will learn how to set your kids up for life and teach them to do it for themselves. I'll outline other valuable parenting and money experiences, like when I learned first-hand that an hour at the local playground is often more valued by children than a world trip, saving all parents a lot of money and emotional energy.

There's even more: I'll answer some of the questions I regularly get asked, like should I invest in shares or property? Is an Airbnb property really a good idea? We will talk about wealth parties, pools and Porsches. I will share a magic trick to turn $1 into over $700,000 and $500 into nearly $3 million, and you will see how you can earn $100,000 per year for doing absolutely nothing.

With the lessons in this book, you can learn how to feel truly happy and calm within yourself and your relationship, and avoid some of the most common costs that come from poor financial management in a household or family. Strap yourself in and get ready to discover a better way for parents and families to achieve not only financial success and greater wealth, but also a happier and more fulfilling life.

PART ONE
CONFUSION TO CLARITY

Feeling confused and unclear is not a pleasant way to be. Whether it's in regard to your money or any other area of life, being in this state will not allow you to achieve the outcomes you want because things become a blur with no direction and purpose.

To move from confusion to clarity, you need to have the right systems and steps to follow, so I have created a range of useful tools for you to use. The benefit of following these processes is that you will clearly see where you are at, where you want to go and the most effective way to get there.

Before reading further, find out exactly where you are at by going to www.thefamilyfinanceguy.com.au and filling out our free financial and fulfillment score-card. This will help you see opportunities and guide your focus areas for success as you read. You will also receive a free personalised results report.

This will take a weight off your shoulders and mind as you will no longer be pulled down by the uncertainty of the unknown. Moving into this mindset will allow you to visualise which things are most important to you and your family, and put your energies and money towards achieving them.

1
Methods And Models
For Your Success

When you have a lot going on, your mind can become a swirling mess of thoughts, activity and busyness. When this is the norm and everyday life, it can be energy sapping and lead to burnout or lost motivation.

I have created a simple method and model that bring structure to the chaos. They are based around the areas I have identified as the most common pressures upon or mistakes made by hundreds of parents and families who are trying to juggle various competing demands.

Using them allows you to see things more clearly and recognise the stresses, pressure points and inefficiencies along with the energy, time and money you're wasting on things that aren't positively enhancing your life or financial outcomes. They will help you change your current approach and build a completely new way of doing things. All the information is here for you: what to do, how to do it and how to keep doing it over and over consistently to enjoy the life you want.

Don't strive for perfection

Here is a great quote that is most commonly attributed to the French philosopher Voltaire:

'Don't let perfect be the enemy of good.'

You may be achieving many good things in your life. Perhaps your career is going great guns with promotion after promotion or your business is growing rapidly. If you have a partner or spouse, they too might be kicking some goals – maybe they are doing really well with their health and fitness. Your kids might be thriving at school and getting excellent grades, but across your life overall as an individual, perhaps part of a couple and a member of a broader family, would you give yourself a ten out of ten? Are you sure you're experiencing all the things you would love to be feeling, doing, achieving, having and enjoying?

It's probable that you will score some areas lower than others because there is so much going on in your life. The idea of getting all areas to a ten likely feels impossible. You know why? Because it probably is, or if it is achievable, it's unlikely to be sustainable across every part of your life. That's what life is, right? An ongoing fluctuation of ups and downs, successes and failures (lessons) and different challenges thrown at individuals and families.

Perfect is simply not achievable for every person in a family, at all times, across all aspects of their lives. Instead, I encourage you not to strive for perfection in anything, whether it's as an individual, a couple if you're in a relationship or with your kids. If you do have it in one area, it is likely to come at the cost of another vital component of your life. Aim for as close to ten out of ten as possible in multiple areas. Not just money; not just health; not just your relationships or career; all of them. Achieving your maximum across numerous areas is not easy, but it is much easier when you do away with the mindset of trying to be perfect.

My aim is not to make you elite at one thing. I challenge you to be great at a lot, but perfect at nothing. I want you to be very good at many things all at the same time. If you can do this, you will enjoy a much more fulfilling outcome for your whole family.

Let go of the idea of perfection. Your busy life doesn't cater for it. Stop trying to dominate in one area and starving others of attention and success. This will allow you to truly achieve the financial, family and life outcomes you desire.

You may have heard of the 80:20 Rule, also known as the Pareto Principle.[1] This states that approximately 80% of outcomes will come from 20% of causes, or the 'vital few'. On the other side of this, 20% of outcomes are the result of 80% of causes.

The 80:20 Rule was first observed by an Italian civil engineer, economist and sociologist Vilfredo Pareto in the early 20th century. He noted that 80% of the land in Italy was owned by 20% of the population, further discovering that a similar distribution existed in other countries as well. Since then, studies have shown that the 80:20 Rule applies in many other areas: in natural phenomena, business, health and productivity. It's a useful lens to assess and measure the results you are getting against the tasks and effort you are putting into different areas of your life, including money.

What 20% of activities generate 80% of your results? What are you doing for the other 80% of the time that may only contribute to 20% of your success, either financially or otherwise? Taking this further and pivoting it slightly, look at it from the point of view of the perfect versus good mentality. If you could be at an 80% success level (eight out of ten) consistently and simultaneously across all key areas of your life while only putting in 20% of the effort you're currently expending to achieve it, imagine how amazing, fresh and energised you would be feeling.

---

1   Tardi, C, '80-20 Rule' (Investopedia, 11 March 2022), www. investopedia.com/terms/1/80-20-rule.asp, accessed 18 May 2022

While this is perhaps stretching the principle a little, it brings us to two key points:

1. With so much to juggle, don't try to be perfect at one thing and fail dismally at many others. It is those failures that can unravel everything. Instead, aim for eight out of ten and balance this across the board on a sustainable basis.

2. If you can put in less time, effort or money (for example 20% of your current rate) to achieve 80% of the results you want, this is an easy and efficient way to run your life. Analyse opportunities to function in this way. I'll outline how time and compounding are great examples of achieving more while having to put in less effort.

The Parental Balance Model

In the introduction, I described busy working parents as jugglers, but the reality is even harder than that. We're more like juggling tightrope walkers. At the end of each tightrope are two separate demands, battling it out to lead us to something we can only have so much of.

While each tightrope is challenging on its own, they all overlap and fight for our attention, energy and money, dragging us down. When it all starts to get too hard, we generally have two options.

The first is to make a drastic lifestyle change. For example, move way out into the bush and live off grid; leave our career or business; stop engaging in everyday life or the community; stop watching the news or using mobile phones and technology. Just a step away from the busy world we are accustomed to creates simplicity and ease in our lives. There will be fewer pressures and many of the demands will slip away.

Some people do this, but it doesn't suit the life most of us want or envisage for ourselves or our children. We may have career or business requirements. Our kids have education needs, family and friends they want to see and various activities or events they enjoy on a regular basis.

Option two is to get clear on what we are fighting against and move from a pushing and pulling approach into smooth, stable and even flow. All of the opposing tightropes will still be there, but we become more adept at balancing on them and working with them. This set of tightropes is depicted by the Parental Balance Model.

The parental balance model is represented in the following graphic.

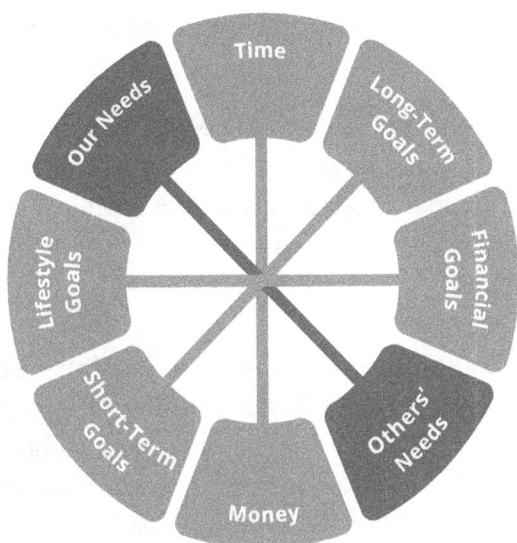

The Parental Balance Model

As you can see, the tightropes in the model connect:

- Lifestyle goals and financial goals – balancing these is always a challenge.

- Time and money – these two aren't necessarily wrestling each other, but they tend to be the most in-demand and under-pressure areas in our lives. Time and money are both finite and sometimes it seems like everyone and everything wants a piece of them, so they often seem in competition.

- Short-term goals and long-term goals – these could be goals of any kind where there is a conflict between what you want now versus long term in an area of your life. In this book, we will focus on short-term and long-term lifestyle and financial goals.

- Your needs versus others' needs – commonly, the 'others' list is quite long. It might include your parents, extended family, certain friends, but in this book, we will focus on 'others' as being your partner if you have one and your kids.

This, of course, is not an exhaustive list of all the things we are managing each day, but it covers the overarching areas that I have found to be most common for busy families. Each area will have underlying subsets and specific items.

For example, the demands on our time in just one day could be go to work, drop off the kids, cook dinner, pay some bills, exercise, call a friend or family member, mow the lawns etc. We could make similar lists for each end of each tightrope, but that would become too difficult to manage.

This is the whole point of the model. If we were to visualise and try to de-pressurise all of our daily requirements and duties, our bodies and minds would implode. That's where many people go wrong. Instead, the Parental Balance Model simplifies it to encapsulate and show the typical needs and wants of busy parents. Then we are better able to visualise what is creating the different points of friction and stress and tackle it with clarity and a structured approach, instead of the day-to-day whirlwind of things to consider. This takes us up to a higher level where we can picture ourselves hovering above the model, looking down into our core areas of focus.

Take a few minutes to look at the model and each tightrope. While it is a balancing act and there is still a lot to deal with, these are *the only things* you need to control and manage to achieve success across all the key areas of your family's life. It can be done, probably more easily than you think. If you follow the advice in this book, I am confident you will do it.

The SELF Method

The Parental Balance Model helps you see the key areas where you need to achieve balance, but the method to successfully do that is the Structural, Emotional, Lifestyle and Financial (SELF) Method. It is so named as your 'self' includes all the things that make you, your life and your goals unique.

It's vital that anything you do is focused on you. Not your friend or your neighbour or a sibling or a work colleague. This is why I developed the SELF Method and why it will work for you – the proof is right there in the name. The method and its underlying models will give you a clear system and decision-making framework.

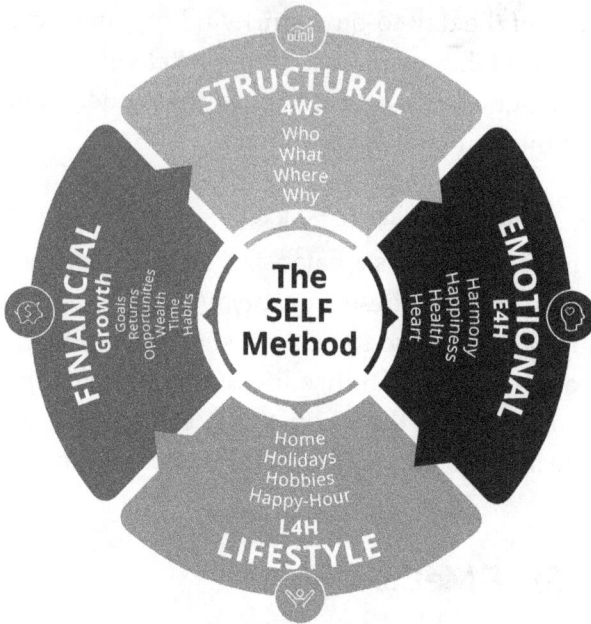

The SELF Method

The SELF Method provides you with four core areas to focus on:

- **S**tructural covers the 4Ws – who, what, where and why

- **E**motional covers the emotional 4Hs – harmony, happiness, health and heart

- **L**ifestyle covers the lifestyle 4Hs – home, holidays, hobbies and happy-hour

- **F**inancial covers the GROWTH acronym – goals, returns, opportunities, wealth, time and habits

The SELF Method comes together as this connected set of four sectors. This combination across different life areas ensures you not only achieve financial freedom and wealth, but also a calm existence and good night's sleep. A better relationship with your family. More of the things you love, fewer things weighing you down and a better life overall.

You can tackle all areas of the method at once, or focus on a certain section or sub-section, but once you and your family have the SELF Method in place, you will enjoy a life that's both rich and enriched.

Let's get started.

Summary

The Parental Balance Model reduces the stresses and anxieties that come from having a lot of competing demands placed on you. By employing this model, you can identify the things you really need to manage and approach them more calmly.

The SELF Method will ensure you know what to focus on to achieve success across the areas you have identified in the Parental Balance Model. It gives you the structure and models to follow to ensure you stay on track, don't get overwhelmed and achieve optimum results.

The SELF Method and Parental Balance Model are even more effective if you adopt an 80:20 Rule mindset. Start expending 20% of the effort you're currently using to generate 80% of your desired life and financial outcomes.

PART TWO
THE SELF METHOD – STRUCTURAL

Structure must come first when you're managing money as it provides a firm base and framework that keeps your financial system stable and held together. If you don't get this right first, it would be like constructing a building without the right foundations.

If you have ever walked past a large construction site, you will know the huge scale of what sits beneath a building. This structural preparation work allows the building to be perfectly functional for hundreds of years. You may also have noticed that it seems like the building process is moving slowly when all the structural base work is being done. Then suddenly, in what feels like no time at all, the building is shooting up higher and higher into the air.

A solid structure allows big and rapid outcomes that can be sustained for years on end. An opposite example would be the Leaning Tower of Pisa. Yes, it's still standing, but precariously.

In his best-selling book *The 7 Habits of Highly Effective People*,[2] Stephen Covey advises us to 'Begin with the end in mind'. Focusing on structure first is doing just that.

---

2   Covey, S. R, *The 7 Habits of Highly Effective People: Powerful lessons in personal change* (Simon & Schuster, 2017)

2
Putting Your Structure In Place

It is believed by many that Abraham Lincoln said, 'Give me six hours to chop down a tree, I'll spend the first four sharpening the axe.' Whether or not it was Mr Lincoln or simply a humble woodcutter who made this quote, the principle behind these words applies well when we're creating a sound structure. We need to avoid building our wealth on shallow foundations just as the woodcutter would never go to work with a blunt axe. Our wealth will grow more rapidly with less effort on our part and remains sustainable for the long term if we put in place stable and strong structures first.

That's not to say our structures won't need to change along our journey. As our circumstances change, there will be elements to add, remove or amend, but getting the structural components in place right from the start is a key factor in achieving optimal results.

Structure must come first. Don't run off and buy investments or get caught up in big ideas before you have done your preparations and set your firm foundations in place. It is better to spend some time at the outset getting things prepared wisely so you can then enjoy ongoing success.

The first thing you have to do is ask yourself the 4Ws.

Who, what, where, why?

The 4Ws structural model – who, what, where, why? – makes it easy for you to understand and remember the key elements that make up the framework for your financial management.

Who refers to the different people or entities that own or hold your financial items. This could be you, your spouse or partner, your children, a trust, a retirement savings structure, a company, a business and so on. Who holds the assets, liabilities or responsibility for the relevant financial items in your life? It is vital that you truly understand who owns what and how, and what role they play in the structure of your finances.

The main reason this is important is for asset protection, tax minimisation and effective management of the asset. You must know who the owner is and the pros and cons of each owned entity, so if you don't already, I urge you to find out.

What has two parts in this model. Firstly, there's 'What?' from a financial perspective. What do you own? What are your assets? What do you owe (debts and liabilities) and what is their value?

The second 'what' is what do you want? You may have heard Simon Sinek recommending we *Start With Why*,[3] which means we focus on why we do something and use that as the motivation to achieve it. It makes a lot of sense and is definitely relevant in the context of this book, but instead of why, here we are focusing on what. If you don't know what you want to achieve, it's like trying to get to an unknown destination with no GPS. You will feel lost and simply never get there.

Most people have no idea what they truly want, or if they do, it's a vague notion floating around in their head and causing confusion. It's vital to have clarity on what you want as you can then set structures to achieve it.

Where is everything? What folder or website or login or bank or insurance company or financial institution is everything held with or in? If I asked you to show me all of your key financial details and documents,

---

3   Sinek, S, *Start With Why: How great leaders inspire everyone to take action* (Portfolio, 2009)

would you be able to do it? Most people either can't or take hours to pull it all together.

It's not just about you knowing, either. Are other relevant people aware of where everything is? For example, do you manage all the finances so your partner has no idea where things are? Do your kids know? Does the executor of your will know? What about your lawyer, accountant, financial advisor and so on?

You and other key people need to know where everything is.

Why is everything currently set up the way it is? Does it make sense for it to continue that way? Why have you done it like this? As your circumstances have changed, have you reviewed it and made amendments to achieve better outcomes?

It can be easy to leave things as they are. It saves the hassle of change, but sometimes things need an update. The reason why you did something a certain way in the past may not be relevant now.

For example, a client of mine had the same investment account for twenty years. It had been appropriate when they set it up and had remained so for years, but more recently, this client had had kids, achieved a higher income and was paying greater taxes. It made sense to set up a new structure to help with tax minimisation and planning for their kids' future needs.

When we analysed the potential difference between the current versus new option, it projected a better outcome of more than $100,000 over time, with no additional level of savings or investment.

Ask yourself why everything is set up the way it is and make amendments if there are benefits to doing so.

Avoid distraction

If structure is so important and makes so much sense, why is it so hard to set up and maintain? The answer is simple: money. Weird, right? To have more money, we need structure, yet the reason we can't have structure is because of money.

Money drives so much in the world; there are plenty of companies and marketing experts that want to do everything they can to get their hands on your share. Don't let them! Be in control; don't let them win. Create your structure and avoid *distraction* at all costs.

Achieving this is now harder than ever before because there are more things to distract our focus from our structure. Online banking, mobile phone apps, credit cards, buy-now-pay-later options, paying via our phone or watch, subscriptions, Uber Eats, retargeting (ads following you based on your previous internet behaviour)… the list goes on. Then of course we have the classic that was around long before technology even existed: keeping up with the Joneses. Many of us feel a need to achieve or better everything our neighbour does or owns, even if we don't like to admit it.

'Too many people spend money they haven't earned, to buy things they don't want, to impress people they don't like.'
— Will Rogers

Please make sure you don't do this. It's just a recipe for unhappiness.

With potentially hundreds of distractions which could prevent us from creating or maintaining structure with our finances and lives, it is critical that we avoid them at all costs. We need to run our own race, but I know it's hard. Distractions are everywhere, so I've developed easy-to-follow wealth wall and wealth machine concepts to help you clarify what you want, get your structure in place and stay focused and on track. More on that in Chapter 3. For now, just take heart from the fact that structure defeats distraction.

Set yourself up for life

I learned from an early age the value of structure around finances. Here's my story of my early days in work.

THE FRUITS OF MY LABOURS

I had my first job was when I was ten. My dad had his own business and, back in the pre-email days, he would post his clients' reports and newsletters. I had to stuff each report in an envelope, lick the flap, stick it down, put the address sticker and stamp on the front, and repeat over and over. I remember my mouth used to get sore and dry from licking the envelopes as I worked my way through these hundreds of letters.

From memory, I got paid 5 cents per envelope, which worked out at around $10 an hour. For a ten-year-old sitting on the couch, probably watching TV at the same time, it was damn good money.

My next job came at age fourteen at the local fruit shop. It paid around $5 per hour, which was a bit rough after my $10 per hour postage career, and it was hard work. Early starts in the cool rooms or lugging 50kg bags of potatoes around the small regional Australian town of Shepparton.

Even though the pay was low, I did as many hours as I could as I liked working. I enjoyed money to spend on clothes, going to the cinema (one of the few things to do in Shepparton) and having fun with my mates. I would also keep some money aside for my goal of buying my first car, which I was able to pay cash for at age eighteen. It was nothing amazing, but certainly better than the average first car.

I remember handing over my hard-earned money and giving the car a big clean and taking it for a spin. That car became my source of freedom, as I moved out of home not long after I bought it to attend university in

Melbourne. I was pretty proud of what all my hard work had got me.

I guess in many ways, the freedom that car gave me is a metaphor for financial freedom. If you work hard, save hard, invest wisely, you achieve this freedom. The ultimate version of that is not having to work for a living. That car didn't take me to the ultimate, but it was my first taste of what increased financial freedom felt like, and I liked it.

With the money rolling in from the fruit-shop job (ha-ha, yeah, right – I keep an old payslip on my desk as a reminder of how little I earned), I started investing in the share market at the age of fifteen. I have always had an interest in finance and growing wealth, which came partly from being naturally good with numbers and enjoying maths more than other subjects, and partly because my dad has been an investment advisor for nearly forty years. I remember having a number of intriguing discussions with him, usually on a car trip somewhere, that made me keen to get involved with investing for myself.

This interest grew when I was completing an Economics and Finance degree at university and learning a lot more about financial strategies and investments. At the same time as university, I was working numerous part-time jobs. I would work in Melbourne during the semester, then during the long summer break, I would go home to Shepparton and work seven days a week for a large fruit cannery. I'm not sure what it was with me and fruit; surely there were easier jobs out there. Again, it was early starts, long days and hard manual work, but it paid really well and set me up for the university year to follow.

Just as I did when I was fourteen, I carried on splitting up my income between meeting my rent and other living costs, enjoying events like overseas trips and music festivals, and putting some away into my ongoing investment account. As my investment knowledge increased, I diligently applied those learnings to my savings month in, month out and things slowly grew.

Broadly speaking, there are three key areas into which we need to be directing funds. I like to give these three areas catchy names – *survival, lifestyle, revival*.

Survival is fairly obvious. It means allocating money to our must haves like a roof over our heads, clothes on our backs and food in our stomachs. Lifestyle covers our wants, not needs. Things such as entertainment and holidays. Revival is where building wealth comes in. By allocating funds to this area, we are improving our fortunes and financial position via the savings and investments we are accumulating and building.

As my income grew over time, I continued allocating to these three areas. I made sure I didn't over allocate to survival and lifestyle – that is called the Income Trap and I will talk about that more in Chapter 12.

Teach your kids structure

You don't need to overcomplicate finances for your children or yourself, but from as young an age as possible, teach them the importance of structure. What key lessons can my story teach your children about money?

Firstly, it teaches them about the importance of hard work. You can always start them doing chores around the house in addition to those they do to contribute to the family. You can pay them for those 'extras' so they learn to earn their pocket money. That then teaches them the value of money.

If kids don't understand that they have to put in the effort required to earn money or they won't have any, they won't learn this valuable life lesson. Getting them to do chores at home in return for a few dollars' pocket money could be one of the most valuable lessons you ever give to your children, but ensure you accompany this with explanations so they connect the two.

When they are old enough, ensure they get a job while still in school. They don't need to do a lot of hours if it doesn't feel right for you or them, but having to go out of the family home to fit into a workplace, learn a job, work well in a team and follow directions from their boss to earn money for themselves will prove valuable to them in so many ways.

Teach your kids to divide their income across survival, lifestyle and revival. A good way to do this is via a percentage-based structure. You and they could agree the split and it will of course change as they get older and become more responsible for the survival elements, but I would aim to get them to start with at least 30% to revival. The percentage approach means as their income increases during their life, they will continue to put a sufficient and significant amount towards growing wealth.

While most parents will pay for the bulk of a child's survival and lifestyle needs, I recommend you ensure they use their own money for some of these things. It could be buying that expensive branded t-shirt they really want, but don't need. It could be meeting their friends for take-out when there is perfectly good food at home. It could be they contribute to the household planning by choosing and paying for some items on the weekly groceries list. Help them see that survival and lifestyle need to be funded from somewhere and they will cope much better when they have substantial life costs like rent and bills in future. When I moved 250 kilometres from home just after my eighteenth birthday to a place where I knew no one, with four years' practice in paying for many things myself, I was well prepared.

As soon as they are old enough to understand, ensure your kids are involved in the administration of the revival element. Giving them the opportunity to learn about how money works and the savings and investments they are growing will increase their knowledge. They will become more attached to the process and reason for putting money aside rather than spending it on whatever shiny item is taking their attention at the time. You can then instil in them a lifetime habit of saving and investing.

With time being one of the biggest aids in growing wealth, if your kids start the revival element from a young age, they could achieve the ultimate financial freedom much earlier than most people. The nest egg they will have built by the time they leave home will give them choices and flexibility during the middle stages of life that most people can only dream of. Without the structure of the survival, lifestyle, revival approach, though, many people will not be allocating funds towards savings and investing.

The retrospective example below shows that if your child allocates just $500 per month to revival, this action alone could turn them into a multi-millionaire.

The chart shows that someone who invested just $500 per month into the Australian share market from 1980 to 2020 would have ended up with an investment worth $2,790,246. While $500 per month × 12 months per year × 40 years = $240,000, this investment turned it into nearly $3 million. This amazing result shows the power of using structure to consistently allocate to revival, not just survival and lifestyle.

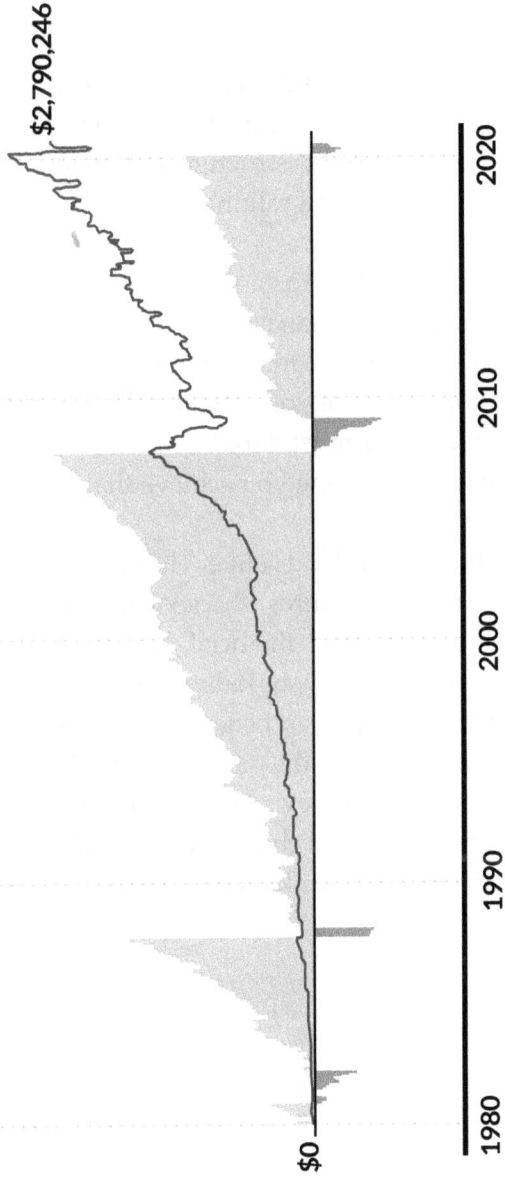

$2,790,246

Bull Years - defined as a price increase of more than 20%

Bear Years - defined as a price decrease of more than 20%

All Ordinaries Index, maximum % change relative to the previous trough (bear years) or peak (bull years)

Return on investment of **$500** each month since 1980 = **$2,790,246**

1980   1990   2000   2010   2020

Growth of $500 pm investment from 1980–2020

Source: Vanguard

Summary

Structure is where everything must start. It is critical and without it you will get nowhere near the optimal outcomes. When it is done right, structure will give you simplicity, peace of mind and calmness.

Start by asking yourself the 4Ws to gain clarity on the key elements of your financial management. This can allow for systemisation so you can put your money management on autopilot. Once you have this clarity, use it to focus yourself. You must avoid distractions and structure is the key to helping you achieve that.

Structure is vital for adults and kids alike. The sooner you implement the right structures, the sooner you can all achieve the lifestyle and financial outcomes you aspire to. Help yourself and your kids. Give yourself the gift of structure so you can benefit from it as soon as possible. Give your kids the gift of doing this so much younger than you so they can reap the benefits throughout their entire life. I challenge you to do it today and set yourself and your kids up for life.

3

The Wealth Machine
And Wealth Wall

D o words like 'budgeting' inflict an immediate
need for sleep, caffeine or alcohol upon you?
Does the mere idea make you feel stressed, bored,
icky, numb or just disinterested? If it does, you are not
alone.

Much common finance terminology evokes negative
thoughts and emotions in people, usually because
such words are associated with hard work and draining processes. Not so in this book. Here, we have a
wealth machine.

Finances should be fun. At the end of the day, they can
create or produce many of the things you want in life.
Say to yourself, 'From now on, I will #makefinances-
fun.' This mindset will make you far more inclined to

engage in the steps you need to gain what you want from your money and make it work hard for you. The wealth machine helps you to achieve this mindset, which can be as simple as changing the words you use. Strap yourself in and get ready to #makefinancesfun.

Key parts to the wealth machine

Like all innovative machines, the wealth machine has a number of parts. They are:

The windscreen

What is this used for? Looking through, of course! We look through the windscreen of our wealth machine and see out towards our vision.

The windscreen has to be the first part of the wealth machine we use. If we don't know where we are going, how can we point the wealth machine in the right direction? The other reason this is vital is because our vision is what motivates us to try harder. It's what gets us out of bed in the morning, engaging in structure and keeping our wealth machine on the right path, avoiding distracting turn offs to roads that are likely just filled with potholes. Distractions on our journey will only slow us down and prevent us from reaching our true destination.

Give your windscreen a try. Take a look out of it. What do you see?

Write down what comes to mind when you look ahead. It can be both the things in your immediate eye line (short-term goals) and those off in the distance that require you to turn on the high-beam lights (long-term goals). What things do you want, desire, dream of for your ideal life and financial position?

Take your time and get everything out. Draw a picture or download a vision boarding app from the app store to help you. Focus on the things that will maximise your short- and long-term outcomes. Once you have written everything down, categorise it into groups. The preferable broad categories would be financial results, family happiness and life balance.

Now put each of the items in those categories into a priority order. Then put a figure for the amount or cost to achieve it next to each one. Finally, put a timeframe next to each one. When do you want to have achieved this item?

For example:

- Goal: grow my investment portfolio

- Category: financial result

- Cost: $1 million

- Timeframe: ten years

An example on my list under family happiness is to do some home renovations. Ideally, I would like to complete these within the next two years and estimate they will cost $200,000.

Keep going to make sure you have your full list, categorised in priority order with estimated costs and timings. It doesn't need to be exact, this is just a rough draft. Keep thinking #makefinancesfun. You are envisioning all the exciting things you want for your money and life.

Finished? Excellent. You now have the beginnings of the roadmap you will drive your wealth machine through over time. If you aren't a car person, the wealth machine can be anything you want. Maybe you love sci-fi – picture it as some amazing machine out of your favourite movie. Maybe you love cycling, running or swimming. Your wealth machine could be a bike or even your body, moving along efficiently and effectively towards your destination. This machine is uniquely yours, so it can be whatever you imagine it to be.

The fuel

Your wealth machine needs a modern, efficient and powerful engine that can really drive you forward to your vision. To make it go, it needs fuel.

Write down all forms of income (fuel) in your house. What hits your bank accounts or life each week or month when you get paid? If it varies or is a bit lumpy (for example, if you are a business owner), estimate the average amount for each period. This doesn't need to be exact. It is just a draft; a starting point; something that feels easy, flows and sticks to the #makefinances-fun mantra.

Got it? Excellent.

All the income you generate is the fuel for your wealth machine's engine. Like an actual engine these days, which could take gas, petrol, diesel, or electricity, your machine could run on a combination of fuels or maybe just one main one. Whatever it is for you is all that matters.

Accelerator

What happens when you put your foot on the accelerator of your wealth machine? You use fuel. If you are the sci-fi wealth machine person, maybe you picture thrusters blowing off. If you are the exercise wealth machine person, maybe you feel your quads burning and the sting of lactic acid as you force out an effort. Either way, the harder you push the accelerator, the more fuel you will use up.

This, of course, is a metaphor for spending money. Write down all the times you push your accelerator in a week or month. What are the things you spend money on? Again, do not strive for perfect accuracy; don't make it a painful chore and go sifting through bank statements or receipts. That will not #makefinancesfun. Think of what you can and get the amounts roughly correct.

Now add up all those items and subtract the accelerator total from the fuel total. Is the result a positive number or a negative number?

If it's a negative number, start walking, because you are out of fuel and your wealth machine is going nowhere fast. That, of course, is not good news. Even if you have a positive number, if it's small, you need to go back and review what you are spending money on and see where you can make changes to create a surplus. Your finances and future lifestyle will go nowhere if you are spending more than you earn. You either need to earn more or spend less, or both.

If it's a fairly high positive number, great. This is called freedom fuel – the fuel left in your tank after you have done all your essential journeys and taken a nice scenic drive past all the things you enjoy doing in life. In other words, it is your ticket to financial freedom.

I spoke about the freedom my first car gave me to get out and about. A well-oiled wealth machine that is functioning smoothly can give you ultimate freedom: financial freedom; lifestyle freedom; freedom of the body and mind. That's the effortlessly light feeling you get when you aren't stressed or constrained or worried by money. Why and how does freedom fuel give you that? Because this is the money you use to grow your wealth.

There is a trick, though – a requirement, actually. Most people make the mistake of using their accelerator willy-nilly, just planting the foot to the floor and heading to whatever feels good. If you do that, you will burn all your freedom fuel and have none left at the end of all your splurting about, so you need to review where you are spending this money. Cut back on things that don't truly matter to you and create more freedom fuel for effective use.

Set the amount of freedom fuel you will save every week or month. Before spending any of it, take that amount out of the equation via a direct debit, not manually. This way, you commit to it and it doesn't take any effort or consideration of whether you will or won't save this week or month.

This approach guarantees your freedom fuel will be there when you really need it, rather than leaving it to chance. Save a set amount, and then spend what's left; never spend and save what's left.

The turbo

Ever been caught behind a slow driver? It's frustrating, isn't it? Don't be that driver with your wealth machine. Yes, drive safely and with appropriate caution, but to paraphrase Mark Zuckerberg, sometimes the biggest risk you'll take is taking no risk at all.

A common mistake people make is not putting their freedom fuel to work for them. They might be great at saving, but not at investing. You will not get wealthy by leaving all of your freedom fuel sitting in the bank. Banks make billions of dollars for a reason: they pay you relatively low rates of interest on your savings and use your funds to generate a greater return for themselves. Would you rather lend your money to the bank (using savings accounts and term deposits) or own part of numerous quality companies and share in their profits? Owning has historically proved much more lucrative than simply saving, so strap a turbo to your money by investing the funds you set aside wisely. You will find plenty of tips on investing in Chapter 11.

The critical components

All power and no control will send you spinning off course, so two of the most critical parts of the wealth machine are the steering and the GPS.

Steering

You must steer the fuel and surplus funds through your machine in the most effective way. I recommend dividing them between these areas:

- Daily life – this is any money you spend on a regular (ie monthly or more frequently) and recurring basis.

- The big stuff – funds for less regular large spends go here, ie things that need to be paid less frequently than monthly. For example, house insurances and rates, utility bills, car registration and insurances.

- Fun – have a pool of money called 'Fun'. Have a fun account for yourself and if you have a partner, encourage them to open one too. You then decide an amount that goes into that account each period. Spend this how and when you wish, but make sure you only continue to pay in the allocated amount, regardless of whether you spend it all at once or not.

- Holidays – who doesn't love a good holiday? There are few better feelings than knowing you have money saved for the next trip or, even better, having it booked and paid for in advance. Holidays are a vital chance to recharge, reconnect as a family, wind down and relax, so set money aside for this to ensure you benefit fully. This avoids the costly mistake of borrowing for a holiday, which is not a good financial decision.

- Buffer – this is not a necessity. If you want minimal accounts, the previous four are the essentials and you could keep a savings buffer in your big-stuff account. The buffer amount is for when an unexpected large cost comes up, for example the whitegoods blow up or the car refuses to start. Everyone's buffer amount will be different depending on the amount that makes them comfortable.

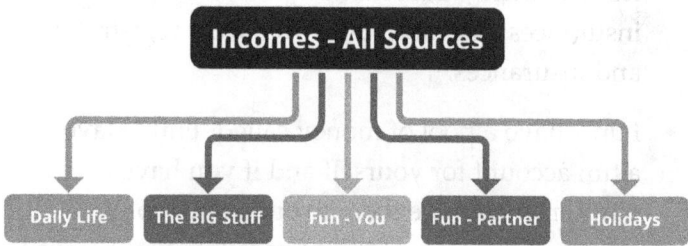

```
                    Incomes - All Sources

Daily Life   The BIG Stuff   Fun - You   Fun - Partner   Holidays
```

Suggested way to steer your money

It's worth noting that loan repayments (if applicable) may come from either the daily life or big stuff account. Generally speaking, making repayments frequently, eg weekly instead of monthly, can create significant interest savings over the life of your loans, so I advise you to speak to a mortgage broker or someone at your bank about this. Seriously, do it! You could be taking years off your loan and making hundreds of thousands of dollars in savings.

While they aren't accounts as such, what about credit cards or store cards or things like buy now, pay later? These, of course, should be avoided; they are just money traps that will end up costing you a fortune in fees and interest. Even if you believe you get great points and rewards on your credit card, trust me. Only a small percentage of people manage credit cards in a way that means they win financially from using them, rather than the bank or rewards provider.

The GPS

This has two functions. The first is to direct your money to places in a smooth and simple way. Wherever you can, use automation such as direct debits, recurring payments, technology or other tools. These tools put the movement of your money and your wealth machine on autopilot, while human intervention generally means things get forgotten or missed or you won't stick to your plans. It is also a whole lot more work that you likely don't need. Have all your income sources go into the daily life account, and then set up a series of direct debits to disperse set amounts to the other accounts on a weekly, fortnightly or monthly basis.

The second role of the wealth machine's GPS is to show you where you are at the start of and throughout your journey. The first co-ordinates for your GPS are, of course, where you are starting from. How do you find this out?

Write down all of your assets by name and value, for example: home, $1 million; bank savings, $20,000; investment portfolio, $400,000; retirement savings, $390,000 etc. Now write down all of your debts and liabilities, for example: mortgage, $270,000; credit cards, $2,350 etc. Subtract your debts from your assets and this is your net wealth. Now you know your current net wealth, if you haven't done so already, write down what you want your future net wealth to be and by when.

Tracking your progress towards your goals on a regular basis is vital. I recommend doing a detailed check every three months. This helps you see if your energy and money are going towards the things you said you really wanted. Are you getting more of those things? Are you making inroads? If yes, it will serve as a nice boost and motivation to keep going. If not, you can steer things back on path to your vision.

It's also vital to track the value of each asset and debt every three months and update your net wealth figure. I recommend tracking your loan to value ratio (LVR) for your overall position. This is the percentage of debt you have compared to assets.

For example, if you have $500,000 of debt and $1 million of assets, your LVR will be ($500,000 / $1 million) × 100 = 50%. This can help you see if your wealth is growing due to increased asset values, decreased debt levels or both. It can also help you keep your risk and debt levels at an appropriately balanced amount – an amount that can assist you in growing wealth, but is not so excessive, it is causing stresses and potential problems. The process of recording everything in a document, spreadsheet or app and updating it regularly to track your position or replot your GPS takes around five to ten minutes. I'm sure you can find five minutes every three months.

Building your wealth wall

There are a number of different contributors to our financial resources over time: some big, some small, some regular and some irregular. These can all be sources of fuel for the wealth machine.

As we've already discussed, it's vital we don't just burn all our fuel. We need to have some control over our accelerator to ensure we have as much freedom fuel left as possible, but fuel can be hard to see. How else can we envision what we are growing and how we are tracking it?

There's an old science experiment you may have done at school. You get a big container and put three different types of rock in it. There are large rocks, medium-sized rocks and small rocks – I am going to call them boulders, rocks and pebbles. Picture these different-sized rocks in your head.

First, load the container up with the big boulders. It looks to be full pretty quickly. Not many boulders fit in before the container is stacked up to the top and out wide to the edges.

If you look more closely, you will notice there are gaps in between some of the boulders where you can put rocks. The overall volume of the container is greater than just the space the boulders are filling.

Now you've filled the gaps with rocks, the container's full, right? No, it's not. If you then pour pebbles over the top, they will flow down into all the cracks and crevices between the boulders and rocks, and the total amount you can fit in the container increases again.

Think of your sources of money as these types of rock. All are different volumes and sizes, but all are important. For example, boulders could be large lump-sum amounts you come into on an irregular basis, perhaps an inheritance, a large annual bonus from your employment, or paying a distribution out of your company at the end of a successful financial year.

Rocks are smaller amounts, but still a good size and they're likely to occur more regularly. For example, your ongoing salary or regular employment income.

Pebbles are even smaller amounts and could be regular or irregular. For example, your annual tax return. The key thing is acknowledging and harnessing all the forms of money that come into your life and putting them towards your vision. Often, many small, medium and large amounts can fizzle away due to a lack of structure, but you can avoid this.

A great way to get motivated to do this is to think about how you can turn $1,000 into $1 million. Sounds crazy, right? How can you turn that small an amount into $1 million? The first thing is to realise that $1 million is just $1,000 x 1,000, so if you can get 1,000 influxes of $1,000, you will be a millionaire.

Visualise and work towards the achievement of this by building a wealth wall. You need 1,000 bricks worth $1,000 each to have your $1 million wealth wall. Now you have rocks and bricks – nice and easy to remember.

Below is an example of a partially built wealth wall. You could create your own version and fill it in as you progressively grow your wealth. If you already have more than $1 million, then use it to track your progress to your next million.

Breaking a big goal like saving $1 million down into 1,000 small goals makes it much more achievable. Give it a try. You can build a wealth wall with some example numbers as everyone's situation is different. Let's get building!

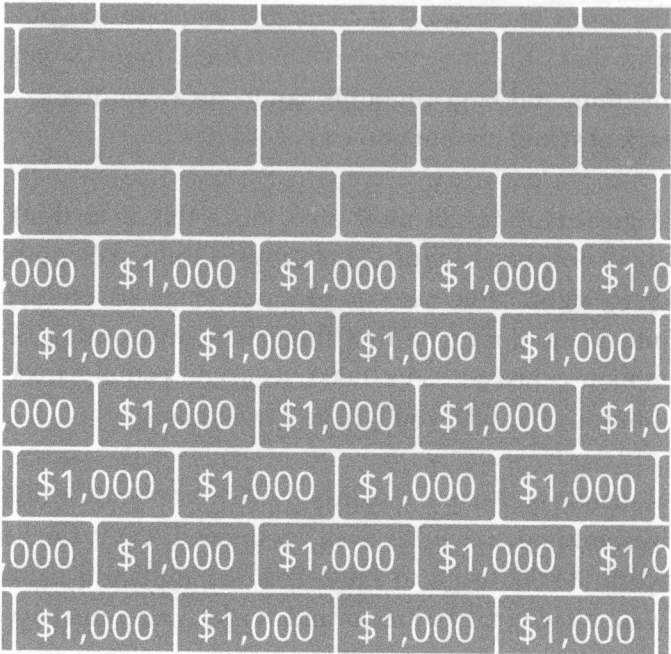

Example of a wealth wall – build 1,000 bricks worth $1,000 each

Example couple's income:

- Weekly after-tax salary partner 1 –
  $1,500 × 52 weeks = $78,000

- Weekly after-tax salary partner 2 –
  $1,000 × 52 weeks = $52,000

Funds available for bricks:

- Assume with good structure, they save/invest
  20% of above income = $26,000

- Annual after-tax bonus partner 1 = $3,000

- Annual after-tax bonus partner 2 = $1,000

- Annual tax-return payment partner 1 = $2,500

- Annual tax-return payment partner 2 = $1,500

- Sell unwanted items = $500

- Income from side business/passion project = $2,000

Total annually = $36,500

Times thirty years = $1,095,000

In this example, two people raise $1 million and still have 80% of their income to use for lifestyle purposes. It assumes no pay rises, investment returns or inheritance comes in, ie no big boulders, which over thirty years would significantly grow the amount. It also doesn't include the value of any existing savings, investments, properties, retirement savings or other assets; this is just a bonus $1,095,000.

It's easy to build a $1 million wealth wall and it's even easier to build one worth much more than that. For example, what if we took that $36,500 per annum and invested it as per the $500 a month for forty years? We would be talking many millions then.

In the example, you can see the different types of rocks used to create the wall. Selling unwanted items is the pebbles and the ongoing saving of salary and tax returns is the rocks; I have deliberately excluded any boulders to show that you can achieve all this without an unexpected big windfall. If that comes, great, but don't pin your hopes on it.

Take actions that are in your control and combine them to create a big outcome. Capture the pebbles and rocks regularly and put them towards effective investments, and let the boulders take care of themselves. Just like a bricklayer physically picks up and stacks each brick, growing your wealth and creating the financial freedom you want is in your hands too.

Without structure, a lot of rocks and pebbles will be lost along the journey and your wealth wall will never get finished, so use the thought of receiving $100,000 a year for doing nothing as motivation. It's a simple equation: if you build a wealth wall to an investment of $1 million and it generates a total return of 10% per year on average, then that is an average annual return on your funds of $100,000. While 10% returns are not guaranteed, they're certainly feasible, but it's only possible to enjoy the $100,000 for doing nothing if you have first put the work into creating the $1 million of capital.

Summary

A clear vision of what you want will guide your actions and decision making when you're building your wealth. If you don't already find this idea exciting, then move to a #makefinancesfun mindset via the wealth machine. Get away from any prior misconceptions or stresses that you may have attached to creating wealth or working on your finances.

When you have a clear vision of where you want to go via your wealth machine, make sure you follow your GPS and steer the right amounts into the right places. This is absolutely critical. Be aware of the different types of financial 'rocks' in your life. Don't waste any of them, not even the pebbles as often these can add up to the biggest amount overall. Build your wealth wall one brick at a time, keep a visual of it, track your progress, admire the wall as it grows and keep constructing.

With the right set of goals and structures to take you there efficiently, the sky is the limit for what you can achieve and the wealth and financial freedom you can create.

PART THREE
THE SELF METHOD – EMOTIONAL

We experience many emotions in our day-to-day lives for a diverse range of reasons. There are little things that create big emotions at the time, such as stubbing our toe, the highs and lows of watching our sporting team win or lose, or hearing the kids telling us they know everything. No big deal and short-term stuff, but in the moment, they conjure up strong emotions.

Then there are big, important events and the related emotions: the sadness of a close friend or family member passing away; losing our job or suffering a business failure. Sometimes events can be protracted and lead to ongoing difficult emotions and mental health pressures.

There are also strong emotions tied to money, in many cases negative ones such as stress, worry and tension. Having worked with many people who have a lot of money, I can tell you that these emotions don't go away for them. Sure, they don't have to wonder how they will get by, but they may have people or things placing demands on their time and energy as a result of their wealth.

Money is a weird anomaly. Either too little or far more than we will need in our lifetime can potentially lead to stress and strong negative emotions. It is therefore vital that we learn to make money a positive part of our lives so we can live at peace with it and use it effectively. I call this having a *positive money relationship*. I love this name as it covers not just our individual relationship with money, but also how we can make money function positively in our personal relationships with our family.

At the end of the day, money is simply a tool to help us have more of the things we want. Not just material items, but events, experiences, education, comfort, a better life, an easier life, options, fun, freedom. Looking beyond our own needs, we can use it to help others. Our kids or other family members, or those in need or less fortunate than us. It can do a lot of good.

There are many reasons why people feel negative emotions related to money. These negative emotions are not a good thing and won't enhance your life. In this part of the book, I'll explain how you can create and enhance your *positive money relationship* to substantially improve your happiness as well as grow your wealth.

4
Managing Emotions Creates Success

Emotions are always a big part of our money-making decisions. If you are naturally a spender, it is likely that the excitement and joy of making a purchase is one of your main money emotions. You like to buy things and it makes you feel good. If you are naturally a saver, it's likely you feel a lot of indecision and uncertainty about using money. Should you buy this item? Can you afford it? Do you need it? You may really want it... but no, you won't buy it.

You can probably relate to being either a spender or a saver, although some people will vary depending on the type and size of the purchase. I find it interesting to see how some people love spending on themselves, while others (even savers) are more comfortable to spend if they are buying for someone else.

These varying emotional factors in how you use or spend your money can be confusing enough for you as an individual. Throw them into a relationship between two people with different backgrounds, views and approaches to money and it gets even more complicated. If you are in a relationship with someone and you are both spenders, it's likely your finances won't be in good shape. You may get the short, sharp joys of the purchase, but then have the long, painful emotions associated with credit card debts or other issues that come from overspending.

If one person in the relationship is a spender and the other a saver, this can cause friction and tension due to opposing views and money traits. If you are both savers, this can work quite well both financially and in terms of relationship harmony. You are aligned and won't create financial issues, but it could mean you don't enjoy all the things you truly want in life.

There is no right, wrong or perfect way to be. Like most things in life, there are pros and cons to our different money habits and the emotions that come with them. That said, there is a lot of benefit in analysing what type of person you are when it comes to money. What sort of emotion is it bringing into your life? What positives or negatives are your money-making decisions creating for you and your family?

Money will often create conflicting emotions. Use the SELF Method and the Parental Balance Model to help you process those emotions and make decisions that factor in all the different feelings. With less extreme emotion going on, you will be more able to navigate the various tightropes.

When you're looking to make a lifestyle goal purchase, you are likely to feel excited about the item, but perhaps concerned about the financial implication. When you're saving or investing, you will likely feel good that you are growing your wealth and improving your financial position, but perhaps ask yourself why you can't have a nice car, watch or world trip. When you're building finances for your retirement, you will probably feel good in the knowledge that you are creating a better future for yourself, but may also ask what if something terrible happened tomorrow and wonder whether you should just enjoy life for today.

If much of this sounds familiar to you, it's normal, but it can be frustrating and exhausting. Let's do away with all these conflicting and draining emotions and create confidence and certainty that you are making the right decisions and on the right path so you can enjoy a positive money relationship.

The way to do this is by using the E, L and F of the SELF Method together when you make your plans and financial decisions. The three together spell ELF, so think of this concept as your own helpful little decision-making elf, there to make it easier for you and support you along the way.

Forget what you have learned about money

Who taught you about money? Your parents or other family members? Your friends? Google? The other parents at the school gates? Your neighbours at a barbecue?

There is a long list of ways that most people learn about money. As a general rule, the learnings will not be appropriate. Why? The reasons are many.

Firstly, are the people who've advised you through-out your life money experts? In the majority of cases, no, they aren't. Secondly, do they know or understand your specific circumstances in great detail? Are they in a similar situation to you? Similar income, level of assets or debts, life stage or generation, views on risk, lifestyle or financial goals etc? Are they spend-ers or savers? Are you? Is their advice purely based on the financial element, or are they thinking about the broader impacts? Have they thought about how something might impact your emotions, lifestyle and overall outcomes? Probably not, so whatever they said may not apply to or be the best option for you.

For example, your grandparents may have grown up through world wars and depressions when access to money was difficult and expensive. They saved to pay cash for everything they bought, including their house (which was probably a fraction of the cost of houses today), and almost never ate out or travelled or enjoyed any major lifestyle 'treats'. Is that the life you would want for yourself and your family? I imagine most people would say no.

Saving hard and working hard are two of the most important traits to financial and lifestyle success, but the world is a different place today compared to the last century and that means a different approach in certain areas will get us better outcomes. There are many examples of this, but two simple ones are:

- **Home ownership** – based on the rise in house prices in most parts of the world since our grandparents' days, it would be a long, slow process to save up and pay cash for a house. Australia, for example, has some of the highest property prices in the world, the median price of a house in Sydney being over $1 million. While home ownership is not a requirement, many people do aspire to it, but waiting until you have saved $1 million may not be appropriate.

- **Debt** – as we'll see in Chapter 6, having some debt managed in the right way can be one of your biggest allies in growing your wealth more efficiently. I'm sure many grandparents' advice would be no debt is best.

When you're reading this book, as much as possible, forget any prior money lessons you have received. Read with an open mind and look to learn and apply the methods and models as your new approach to money management and lifestyle planning. At the end of the day, this approach is all about your SELF, so it's aimed at getting you, not your neighbour or cousin, the outcomes you desire.

The costs of not factoring emotions into financial decisions

Emotions are normal. They will always be there and they can be important, so we need to consider them and can't just take a purely financial or dollar view of our decisions.

In this section, we will look at some of the most common costs of not factoring emotions into our financial decision.

Relationship costs

Money is one of the biggest causes of relationship issues. Clearly, couples can get better at how they manage money together – that is the operative word right there: together – but many times, I see one person in the couple with the bulk of the responsibility for managing the finances.

I get that. Busy families need to divide the various responsibilities of the household to be able to conquer them, but couples at least need to be talking about their finances, along with their vision, goals and dreams, on a regular basis. If they aren't, then it's inevitable one or both partners will start to feel like they aren't getting what they want from their money or life.

Sometimes, this communication step is the problem in itself. If a spender lives with a saver, for example, whenever they talk about money, it doesn't tend to go well. Perhaps one person in a relationship just finds money confusing or stressful, or they have no interest in it. Every conversation on the subject turns into a disagreement, so they go there less and less until they hardly ever speak about it at all.

If this resonates with you, I guarantee if you and your partner bury your heads in the sand and never resolve your financial differences, it will not end well. To avoid the relationship costs of not factoring your money emotions into your lives, it is vital you have great ways of communicating and dealing productively with your finances together.

Here are some tips to help you achieve this:

1. Use the #makefinancesfun mantra as the basis for your communication.

2. Be aware that each of you will have different backgrounds, views and emotions around money, so be patient and understanding of each other.

3. Analyse if you are spenders or savers (as individuals and a couple), and talk about that and how to manage those potential differences effectively. There is no right or wrong way to be, but talking about this will likely lead each of you to move slightly towards the other's end of the scale, find a better middle ground and enjoy the benefits of this. For example, the spender may become more of a saver and feel greater financial security. The saver may feel more excited and invigorated about their lifestyle as they engage in the things they love by spending a little on what's important to them.

4. Have wealth parties – more on this in Chapter 12.

5. Show unexpected acts of kindness and generosity towards your partner through random acts of kindness (RAKs). As money can create tension, RAKs can break that down and act as a feel-good relationship booster.

THE POWER OF RAKS ON MY EMOTIONS, RELATIONSHIP AND MONEY

I had a pretty weird but cool experience of the power of RAKs myself. I was listening to a book on this subject called *Letting Go* by David R Hawkins,[4] which was talking about how we need to show compassion, care and kindness to others.

---

4   Hawkins, D. R, *Letting Go: The pathway of surrender* (Hay House, 2014)

That day, I set about living this way. I decided I would put a lot of effort into tidying our yard so it would look nice for when my partner got home, so I went out and bought a new line trimmer and got to work.

The trimmer needed special fuel, so I went to the service station. I had to take my partner's car as she was using mine, and as I got back in after buying the trimmer fuel, I noticed her petrol tank was about half full. The car was definitely not in need of any petrol, but it was another opportunity to try my new life lesson out. By filling up her fuel tank, I hadn't done something that was urgent or a necessity, just a nice gesture focused on the RAK mindset. Having done something nice for her that would make her life a little bit easier, I felt good. I didn't even tell her; the warm feeling of knowing I had done it was more than enough reward for me.

As I went to step inside the car, I saw a $100 note sitting at my feet. I picked it up, looked around to see if anyone had dropped it, checked that it was real, and then went on my way.

I was blown away. It was as if the life lesson I was only listening to an hour earlier had immediately shown itself to me and said, 'Yes, I am real, now keep living this way.'

I decided to take things a bit further. When my partner got home that night, I handed her the $100 note and told her to go and do something nice for herself with it. She was so excited and grateful, and loved this random gift she could spend on whatever she wanted.

That series of events was a great life lesson for me, and hopefully it will give you some ideas of how to improve your life through RAKs. Don't do RAKs to get anything back, but you might be surprised by how good it'll make you feel.

Financial costs

When we don't feel good about something, we tend to avoid it and not give it much energy. We might be able to grind through and focus on it for a short period of time, but we will struggle to make this habitual and ongoing.

A good example is health and fitness. Often, people will start a new diet or gym routine and go really hard at it for a couple of weeks, but they aren't approaching it in a sustainable way. They are overdoing it, so it feels hard and unenjoyable, and in time they drop off and go back to their old eating habits and couch-potato lifestyle as the emotions surrounding exercise and healthy food aren't positive.

The same thing can happen with money. If we aren't feeling good about money or investing or dealing with our finances, we will spend less time doing it. If we aren't seeing progress or enjoying the things we want for our life or money, then we won't want to put effort into it. But like no one stays healthy for life by eating well and exercising for only two weeks, our money won't stay healthy if we only give it the odd bit of attention or a short new-year's resolution level of effort.

It is important to recognise and acknowledge if this is the case for you. Are you feeling average about money or that dealing with it is hard work? Are you avoiding it as a result? If you are, please don't keep doing this. Face it, otherwise you will never achieve your potential in regard to the financial outcomes you truly want and can achieve.

Once you face it and own it, you can change your emotions around money by using the tools and techniques in this book to make it a positive part of your life. Not only will you feel better, but you will avoid the financial costs of not creating a positive money relationship.

Environmental and social costs

In today's society, we have much greater awareness about the environmental impact of our decisions. As a parent, you likely care about what your decisions might mean for your children or grandchildren in the future. One of the great evolutions of investment markets is the way they now consider environmental, social and governance (ESG) factors.

When you look at companies you might invest in, you can screen out certain factors. This allows you to feel positive about what the companies you do invest in are doing in regard to ESG when they manage their organisation and operations. By having a strong set of ESG screens across your investments, you can have greater confidence that you are investing in ethical businesses that will hopefully create a better future for your children and grandchildren. You can factor your ethics and emotions into your money management and investments and feel more positive about what they are supporting, which enhances your desire to understand them. If you know your money is having a positive impact on things that are important to you via your investments, then you are more likely to carry on investing in that area.

Today, global sustainable fund assets have grown to be a significant portion of all investment assets. Clearly, this is a big focus for people, and not only is it good for the world, it can be good for your desire to invest and grow your wealth.

Resolving your stresses and anxieties

What are your main stresses? They could be financial or non-financial, but grab a piece of paper or open a document and write them down.

Did you really write them down? Please do, it's important.

OK, how did you get on? What is on your list? What's causing you to feel stressed or anxious?

Now categorise each item on your list into stresses you would associate with money and those that aren't about money. You could simply write an M next to the ones that are money related and NM next to the ones that are not.

When you've done this, take another look at the list. Are the stresses related to you personally or someone else, for example the kids or another family member?

While none of us want stresses in life, they are unavoidable. We will never have no stresses or road bumps; it's about managing and minimising them rather than thinking we can avoid them.

To help minimise your stresses, there are a few things you can do. First of all, write them down and categorise them as explained above. You will then be clear on what is stressing you out, whether it's a financial or non-financial stress and whether the stress is about you as an individual or about someone else important to you. When these things are clear, it helps you to break each stressor down and deal with it.

For financial stresses, analyse whether you are in control of the stressor or not. For example, you may have borrowed too much money and be stressed about how you will pay it back, or maybe you made some poor investment or money decisions and you are worried about the impact they will have. These are things that are in your control – you made the decisions. On the flipside, a common financial stress that is out of your control is losing your job or business as a result of the economy not going well.

It is important to categorise your financial stresses this way because you don't want to spend too much time or energy focusing on things you can't control. You simply need to manage your way through them.

Focus your energies on the stresses you can control. What's done is done, so let it go; you can't change the past. Move on so you don't allow a poor decision to have a detrimental impact on your future life or financial position. David Hawkins's book *Letting Go* is really helpful for processing something that is now in the past and won't serve you well if you carry it into the future.

Understand how the mind works and what causes stressful and anxious thoughts and emotions. In other words, understand why we as humans worry. Worry is natural and goes back thousands of years into human evolution. For a simple lesson on why we have these feelings, why most of the ways we try to fix them just make them worse and how to fix them, I highly recommend *Don't Feed the Monkey Mind* by Jennifer Shannon.[5]

---

5   Shannon, J, *Don't Feed the Monkey Mind: How to stop the cycle of anxiety, fear, and worry* (New Harbinger, 2017)

For stresses that aren't caused by you or aren't yours as an individual, use the 'our needs' versus 'others' needs' tightrope of the Parental Balance Model.

Our Needs	Others' Needs

Life as a family is always going to be a balancing act of what you want and need and what other members of your household need. Are you getting the balance right? Are things tilted too much in one direction? Do you need to talk about and deal with any stresses (money and non-money) that are coming from others in your life? By being clear on what is at the root of your stresses and considering if you need to put greater time and effort into resolving this, you can better communicate any issues and create a better outcome.

These conversations help you formulate a plan that allows for your individual needs and those of your family members to be met, achieving this with minimal stress. Set plans in place that allow everyone to get as much of what they want as possible. Show them the tightrope to help them better understand the competing demands at play and that it's important things are in balance for you and them. The image of the tightrope gives you a clear visual to base your conversation on.

It's unlikely anyone will get everything they want, and certainly not immediately, but talking about everyone's vision will allow for maximum achievement for all parties and a strong team-oriented approach. If your stresses are related to your children and they are old enough to understand a discussion like this and the concept of the tightrope, involving them can be a great way to help your family have positive and productive conversations not just once, but on an ongoing basis. The fairness and balance of this ensures everyone is getting an appropriate outcome and can agree a way for them to feel their needs are being met.

Summary

Start with a clean slate around how you think about money. Forget the past. The solution to managing your emotions around money is not to ignore them or hope they will go away. Instead, acknowledge them, write them down, face them and talk about them. What are they? Are they serving you or holding you back? Are they impacting your life or your family's life? Bring them out in the open and factor them into your decision making so everything is clear and on the table.

The process of communicating thoughts, feelings and stresses will make everything much clearer and help you make better financial and life decisions as an individual and family. Then you can minimise some of the common costs of not factoring emotions into your financial decisions. Use the ELF elements of the SELF Method and the Parental Balance Model to assess the emotions you are feeling about different areas of your life, money and decisions. They will help you consider whether a certain decision will enhance enough key areas and people to make it the best outcome.

This process allays some of the fears and stresses you may be feeling around money and other areas of your life as you will know that you have applied a strong process and reasoning behind what you are choosing, rather than simply letting emotions control the decision. In this way, you can remove negative money emotions, be more at peace with your money management and decision making, and have a set of tools to discuss and agree what is best for yourself and your family based on your situation and vision.

5

The Emotional 4H Model

I have worked over the years with many people who have substantial amounts of wealth and some have now been clients for more than fifteen years. We meet regularly, sometimes in their homes, and talk about everything happening in their lives, not just their finances.

Reflecting on my interactions with wealthy people across a range of personality types, I can assure you that money alone does not make them happy. Many wealthy people are happy the majority of the time, but it is a combination of other factors in their lives that determines that happiness, not just their money.

On the flipside, not having money can make people unhappy, but only if they allow it to. Obsessing that having more money will make you happy is a great way to be unhappy, but I have seen people do this to themselves. They focus on the future when they expect to receive a large sum of money, perhaps from an inheritance, and waste the years leading up to that, damaging relationships and their own health, waiting and believing the money will solve their problems.

Oddly enough, whenever I have seen this, the people have been in a comfortable financial position anyway. Not rich, but they have a well-paid job, a good asset base and sufficient money to enjoy a comfortable lifestyle. In some cases, the money they hoped for or expected doesn't come and they've wasted all those years of anticipation for nothing.

Money can give you a better and happier life. It can give you greater options, choices, comforts and experiences. It can make you feel more relaxed, secure and at ease, but it will only enhance your life if you are already in the right state of mind. It will only improve a family who are already happy in each other's company.

A happy and enjoyable life is not determined by money, it is merely enhanced by money, so you need to ensure you are putting the work in to other key areas of your life that will make you feel good. This is why the emotional part of the SELF Method is critical. Hopefully, the financial part will give you all the money and wealth you desire, but you must combine it with emotional success to live the life you truly desire.

Naval Ravikant, an entrepreneur and investor, tweeted that, 'A calm mind, a fit body, a house full of love. These things cannot be bought – they must be earned', and I feel this is very relevant to the emotional model.[6] It's often easy to think the 4Hs will just take care of themselves, but they won't. We need to show our emotions the respect and effort they deserve to ensure we can feel at our best as much as possible.

As the emotional model is made up of 4Hs, an easy way to refer to it is E4H:

- Harmony
- Health
- Heart
- Happiness

Harmony

How grating and uncomfortable is it when even one relationship in your life is not in harmony? It could be a close relationship with your family or child, or with someone not so close like a neighbour or work

---

6   Ravikant, N, (@naval) 'A fit body, a calm mind, a house full of love …' (22 February 2018), https://twitter.com/naval/status/966512979066765313 , accessed 18 May 2022

colleague, but it just doesn't feel right. As a result, it can eat up a lot of your emotional energy and spoil your zest and buzz for life.

When everything is going well, how warm and fuzzy a feeling is that? You are living in harmony with all those around you, so life feels easy and light and comfortable.

Think about any relationships you have right now that are not in harmony. I encourage, or challenge, you to resolve them. Reach out to the person, have a conversation, deal with the issues, big or small. It will take a huge emotional weight off your shoulders, and you can then use the extra energy that generates to create a better and happier life for yourself and all those around you.

Of course, life will throw things at you that may make it difficult to live in harmony at all times. You don't want to become a yes person and let everyone walk all over you or treat you with disrespect. There are times when you need to stand up for what is right and follow your morals and ethics, but particularly in relationships that truly matter to you, disharmony has a negative impact on your life. Take the step of reaching out and resolving any issues, and it will improve your life significantly.

In the last chapter, we looked at the impact money can have on families. If money is having a big negative impact on your relationship harmony with anyone in your family, use the advice in this book to assist you in resolving this, and in turn work better together with the people in your household to have a more harmonious relationship with money. If you have harmony in your life, you will be less burdened by draining issues and the negativity that surrounds them.

If you are in a relationship, a great book to read to aid relationship harmony in general, including around money, is *The 5 Love Languages* by Gary Chapman.[7] It covers money considerations, for example spenders versus savers, and a range of other valuable topics. Understanding harmony for your partner and yourself will allow you to factor this into your overall life, behaviours – including around your finances – as individuals and a couple. Finances can be one of the biggest negative factors impacting relationships, so work in harmony and your finances can function more effectively.

Health

Your diet is not only what you eat; it is what you watch, listen to, read and the people you spend time with. It's important to be mindful of the things you put into yourself in every sense.

---

7   Chapman, G, *The 5 Love Languages: The secret to love that lasts* (Moody, 2015)

Health and money have a lot of similarities. Many people struggle to obtain or retain their health and many people struggle to achieve the same with their money. This is because both require discipline and there are a lot of distractions trying to push us off course.

If we feel flat, we might reach for a sugary treat or an alcoholic drink. If we feel tired, we might reach for the caffeine. These don't help and aren't going to aid our long-term health or energy levels. Even with the good things for our health, we can become overwhelmed by distractions. Should we buy that new piece of fitness equipment, go to the gym, take that supplement? I thought seven-minute abs was good, but now there is six-minute abs. Arrrgggghhhh! Our mind is blown and when we are confused, we tend to give up.

Despite the similarities between health and money, why does a finance book have a section about health? Simple. You can achieve more financial success if you are physically and mentally healthy. If you are healthy, you are more able to function at your best and this will lead to a better life in every way, including financial results.

While I'm not a health expert, I have cracked the code in the context of a juggling tightrope-walking busy working parent of simple and easy ways to be physically and mentally healthy. The great part is you can achieve this by spending minimal time, energy or money, and that's our goal, right? To ease the pressure on the competing demands that make up the Parental Balance Model.

Not only do you need to be healthy to meet all your responsibilities, but I'm sure you would like to feel great, too. Without your health, you have nothing. When you aren't healthy, it doesn't matter if you have $1 or $1 billion, you still feel crap. I am personally passionate about a healthy lifestyle and physical health, but it's only in more recent years that I have learned about the power and importance of good mental health. It can assist our performance in our work, parenting and relationships. If I can pass some of my learnings on to you to improve your life, that is important to me.

For busy parents, improving our physical and mental health needs to be done in the context of what our lives look like and not that of an elite athlete. We are not trying to make the Olympics in terms of our physical performance in one event; we are striving to be Olympians in the most multi-faceted sport in the world: the busy juggling tightrope-walking parent. Even a decathlete cannot compare to that.

Here are some tips I have found to be hugely beneficial. Some I have only employed recently and others I have done for twenty-five years.

Physical health

To be physically fit and healthy, you only need to use your body. Oh, and a pair of shoes is handy. You do not need a $10,000 bike, you do not need hours every day and you do not need a gym, personal trainer or loads of equipment.

The great thing about fitness is it's simple and basically free, so there's a finance tip in itself. You can find a lifetime's supply of expert information about exercise, weight loss or fitness in a myriad of other places, but sometimes a simple piece of advice that's specific to you as a busy working parent can go a long way. There are just two things you need to do.

Firstly, move and strengthen each week. I find I do this most effectively via running (or you could walk if you aren't up to running yet) and gradually increasing your distance and/or speed. Then for strength, I do push-ups, sit-ups and dips, all of which only require my own body weight. I do ten minutes of strength exercises a few times a week and it makes a significant difference.

While there are great benefits from it being a deliberate effort, ie you purposely go out for a walk or run, you can also easily incorporate it into your daily life by walking instead of driving, taking the stairs instead of the elevator etc. A device that counts your steps (most phones offer this now) is great for setting a daily goal.

This will often encourage you to take that after-work or after-dinner walk that you may not have bothered with otherwise.

Physical health comes down to a little effort and wanting to feel good. It does not need to be confusing or expensive.

Secondly, eat real food. I have never dieted in my life and enjoy plenty of 'treats' every week. A piece of cake (my partner is an amazing baker), a cold beer, takeaway night – that's all fine, but in between, eat a balanced diet of real food, minimising sugar and saturated fats. Make yourself aware of how ridiculously bad for you certain things are and avoid them as much as possible.

OK, there's nothing new here. Just a reminder that obtaining and maintaining good physical health does not need to be hard, time-consuming or expensive.

Mental health

For the first thirty years of my life, I would say I had zero mental health considerations. While I always had a busy life and the stress that comes with that, I didn't have any notable issues. Then at age thirty and the few years that followed, a lot more came on to my plate. I took on debt to buy a new home and a business, along with the pressures of being a business owner. I became a father, moved states, created a start-up... the list goes on. Essentially, I had many large life events happening at once and it was stressful. I'm sure you can relate.

What can we do to manage the impact of this stress? As with physical health, I am not a mental health expert either, but through much trial and error and effort, I have found some simple, free and effective ways to ensure a strong, stable and high level of mental health.

To start with, maintain good physical health. This along with regular exercise will have a huge impact on your mental health.

Secondly, minimise alcohol. I have had plenty of big nights out in my life, and occasionally I still will – nothing wrong with blowing off some steam every now and then. There's also nothing wrong with a nice quiet drink at home. I am in no way saying people shouldn't drink at all, but I have noticed a significant improvement in my mental health when I control my alcohol intake in my normal week-to-week life. I have watched this and gauged the impact the amount of alcohol and even the types of alcohol I drink will have on my mental health.

Give it a try for yourself. Even if you aren't a big drinker, do a little bit of tracking how you feel the next day after a couple of alcoholic drinks versus none. No alcohol will likely help your sleep, energy levels, clarity of thought, ability to exercise and many other things. See if some changes to your drinking habits could make you feel a lot better.

What about caffeine? I 100% do not do well when I drink too much coffee. It impacts my sleep, gives me anxiety and just does not make me feel good.

Coffee has been well marketed as the go-to drink if we are tired. Personally, I think it's bad for us. The problem is, many of us (including me) love the stuff. I like the taste, I like having it in my hand while going for a nice walk, I like the idea that it is going to give me a boost, but trial and error has shown me it does little to help me.

Due to its effect on our nervous system and our sleep, caffeine can never have a positive impact on our mental health. Track your mood, energy and sleep levels when you change your caffeine intake. As with alcohol, I'm not saying don't drink coffee at all, but if you are a heavy coffee drinker, give this a go and see what you notice.

Gratitude. I only discovered gratitude four years ago, but since I did, I have practised it every day. It's absolutely amazing and such a powerful way to set my day up for positivity and success. Gratitude is the process of being thankful and showing appreciation. I use an app called 'The Five Minute Journal', but you could simply write down everything you're grateful for.

My practice involves doing this in the morning:

- Writing down three things I am grateful for.

- Writing down three things I will do to make it a great day.

- Writing down affirmations about myself – for example, 'I am enough', 'I am loved'.

It is best to practise gratitude at night as well, but I admit I rarely do this. When life feels hard, busy and stressful, starting your day with gratitude and focusing your thoughts towards all the good things in your life can bring a huge improvement in your mental health.

Another thing that has absolutely blown my mind is meditation. If you are not a spiritual person and find it hard to sit still quietly and are a bit sceptical about things like meditation, then I get it. I was too. I couldn't think of anything worse a few years ago, but now I cannot speak highly enough of the results it produces.

Even if you feel meditation isn't up your alley, please trust me and try it. It is an absolute life changer.

MY MEDITATION JOURNEY

As a kid growing up in a small town thirty-five years ago, I was never exposed to meditation or anything like it, but these days, my kids and many others do meditation in school. How cool is that? It's come a long way, but for me, meditation was so foreign and 'weird' that I sure wasn't going to be wasting my time on it.

When I grew up and had to take on a lot more stress in life, I needed the tools to function well and deal with this stress. Being in a different headspace and adjusting to being a single dad, I wanted to stay physically and mentally healthy so I could be a good parent and keep running my business during a difficult time. That is when I discovered and started practising gratitude and meditation. I'd become more open minded and willing to try things.

How did I get into meditation in the first place? One day, I googled 'life coach' and by chance found one who was about a kilometre from my office. Literally two hours later, she was holding a lunch-time group coaching session. It must have been fate; I was meant to go.

The group coaching session was at her house – at her kitchen table, in fact. There I was, a thirty-five-year-old guy in a suit, drinking tea with four women in their sixties, all of us talking about our life issues and problems. I won't lie, it felt a bit odd and I was a fish out of water, but I fully engaged in the session and it was hugely beneficial.

One of the big things the coach spoke about was her own past. She had been an alcoholic, gone through a divorce with young children and had many demons she'd had to face. Being extremely honest, she went on to explain that the single biggest thing that had turned her life around was discovering and using meditation. It'd had such a big impact on her that she had then spent years learning more about it and honing her practice. She loved it so much she even wrote a book about it called *The Happiness Hunter's Guide to Meditation*. I found her story so powerful that I purchased her book, read it quickly and started doing guided meditations via an app.

I found it helpful, particularly on nights where all my stresses were keeping me awake as there was a meditation that aided falling asleep. I kept using the app for a couple of years, usually around five to ten minutes per meditation, two to three times per week, but over time, I let my meditation practice slip away to once a week at best.

About eighteen months ago, I noticed I was feeling anxious – not something I typically experienced. It manifested as a daily tight feeling in my chest and nothing I did would make the feeling go away. I didn't know what was causing it, but I sure knew I didn't want it there. It made me feel like shit, worried and uncomfortable as I was so conscious of it.

One day at a work meeting, I randomly met Neomal Silva who teaches Vedic meditation, which is a mantra-based practice. No apps or guidance needed. I told him about my brief use of meditation in the past and found his thoughts on meditation and its benefits interesting. He basically told me that Vedic meditation is completely different to guided meditation and could help me with the feeling I was getting, as well as provide a huge number of other benefits. I was sceptical at the cost he quoted, picturing a lot overpriced humming and burning incense. The F of my ELF was kicking in, weighing up if the expense was going to create enough of a benefit to my emotional or lifestyle outcomes.

The next week, I saw a friend who was a big Vedic meditation fan. Hearing her glowing comments about it and its impact on her life, I realised I needed to consider doing this. That same week, I heard Hugh Jackman on the Tim Ferris podcast talking about his daily routine and what helps him to stay fit, healthy, happy and successful as a busy working family man.[8] He spoke of his use of meditation every morning and later in the day. This thing kept popping up in my face and I couldn't deny any more that it was meant to be, so I signed up.

As I was leaving my first session, I felt great. I had discovered something new and different and empowering; something that could definitely have a positive impact on my life. Walking to my car, I was shocked as a bird flew up from under my feet. As it fluttered past my face, it was so close I could feel the air movement from its wings and I realised it was a white dove. I quickly googled what seeing a dove means and discovered that it was sent to remind me to focus on the peace in my heart, which is always present all around me in my life. If that didn't make me (and hopefully you) believe that meditation was definitely a positive thing to add to my life, then nothing would.

Needless to say, I loved completing the course and have since followed the recommended practice of meditating twice per day for twenty minutes at a time. It has had a huge impact on my energy levels, sleep, mood, ability to concentrate, work performance and productivity. It has helped me feel calmer and happier, and the anxious

---

8 Ferriss, T, 'The Tim Ferriss Show Transcripts: Hugh Jackman on best decisions, daily routines, the 85% rule, favorite exercises, mind training, and much more' (#444, 30 June 2020), https://tim.blog/2020/06/30/hugh-jackman-transcript, accessed 19 May 2022

feeling has never come again (unless I drink too much coffee).

Trust me and try meditation. It will change your life.

Do you ever hit an afternoon slump? Feel sluggish around 3pm? Common remedies are sugar or caffeine, but this is a short-term fix and you're likely to be left with a sugar crash or bad night's sleep due to the caffeine. Replace these short-term fixes with meditation.

I've hit the afternoon wall on numerous occasions and it used to lead to a tiring and unenjoyable remainder of the day, but a meditation means I burst back into life and achieve more in a few hours than many could in a whole day. I'm highly focused, efficient and energised. Seriously, this stuff is powerful and worth doing. All of its side effects will have a huge positive impact on your mental health.

Heart

Our decisions are determined by our head and our heart. Having the head involved in financial decisions is important; this can stop us from making the wrong choices and putting ourselves in a bad position. I wholeheartedly support the use of the head as a key part of creating wealth, but the SELF Method has an emotional element to it on purpose. This ensures we take a more balanced approach so we achieve overall life and family happiness, as well as financial freedom.

Use your head, but do not ignore your own and your family's hearts when making financial decisions. What emotional considerations do you need to factor in to life's big decisions? It is about balance. Not all head as that may lead to great financial gains, but emotional downsides. Not all heart, as that could place you in a poor ongoing financial position.

If you are someone who predominantly uses your head in decision making, allow a little more heart into the equation. It's likely to lead to a happier life over-all for you and your family. If you are someone who focuses a lot on the heart, consider whether you some-times need to let the head do the talking to ensure your outcomes are where they need to be.

Be aware of finding the right head–heart balance in your financial decision making as an individual and part of a family. It is sure to create a better set of results for both the short term and the long term.

Happiness

Finish this sentence: *Happiness for me is…* Simply enter the word or phrase that comes to mind at the end of that statement. Do it again and again and again until

you get out all the quick responses about what makes
you happy.

Examples could be:

- Happiness for me is seeing my children play and
  laugh and smile.

- Happiness for me is a walk by the beach.

- Happiness for me is the euphoric feeling just after
  an intense exercise session.

- Happiness for me is snuggling up on the couch
  with a good book or TV show.

- Happiness for me is winning a big client or
  contract at work.

- Happiness for me is feeling financially secure.

- Happiness for me is seeing a big, fat portfolio
  balance and knowing I've built a lot of wealth.

- Happiness for me is the feeling around about day
  three of a holiday where I finally switch off and
  relax.

- Happiness for me is knowing my finances are
  in order and my family and future will be well
  looked after.

- Happiness for me is knowing I have choices and
  options because I have made sound decisions to
  put myself in a great position.

- Happiness for me is feeling physically and mentally fit and strong and not weighed down by worries.

Keep writing until you feel all the examples are out of your head. This should now form part of the vision we spoke about in the context of the windscreen of the wealth machine. If these are all the things that bring you happiness, of course they need to be part of your future life and planning.

Now consider what decisions can bring you the best balance of happiness across all these areas in conjunction with the Parental Balance Model. What actions, both lifestyle and financial, will bring happiness to you and others in the short term and long term?

The lifestyle actions usually exhibit an obvious vision of how to increase happiness as they're often items or experiences that you can see or touch, but don't dismiss the impact of finances on happiness. Keep in mind that wise financial decisions and financial success can bring a lot of happiness as they reduce stress, bringing calmness and a feeling of being on the right path. They also give you choices. Without some smart financial actions and investments, your future and long-term happiness may be negatively impacted.

As a strong financial position can improve your feeling of security and being in control, this helps your mental health. Don't only aim for the short-term sugar hits; focus on the things that will have a truly positive impact on your ongoing happiness.

If finding the time or structure to follow the advice I have shared in this chapter seems difficult for you, a great book to read is *The Miracle Morning* by Hal Elrod.[9] Often, the way we start our day is how we finish it. If we start sluggish and flat, we may struggle to hit a rhythm and feel good throughout the day. Check out Hal's book as a great way to achieve the E4Hs: harmony, heart, health and happiness.

Summary

If we don't have harmony in our heart, health and happiness, then no amount of money will give us an enjoyable life. If even one of those things is not going well, it can be all consuming and take up much of our focus and energy. Ironically, we are likely to have less money if we aren't living in harmony, good health and happiness, and aren't listening to our hearts as well as our heads. This is because we won't be able to function at our best, and our ability to perform well in our different roles in life is what creates the financial resources to build wealth.

It goes without saying that we must focus our attention on things that will ensure we have harmony in

---

9   Elrod, H, *The Miracle Morning: The 6 habits that will transform your life before 8am* (John Murray Learning, 2017)

our relationships, health in our body and mind, and happiness in our heart and home. Without these things, life will be a grind and money will serve little purpose. Money simply enhances an already good life rather than being the thing that gives us a good life.

Assess where you are at with the E4Hs and spend time (and, if necessary, money) to improve them. The payoff from this will be significant in every way, including financially.

6
Changing Your Emotions Around Debt Can Make You Wealthy

Debt often conjures up negative emotions. Even the word itself is unpleasant, four letters that could easily be replaced with plenty of other words of similar length. Keeping it clean (this is a family book, after all), it just feels yuck. We could change 'debt' to 'yuck' and it would work.

Taking on certain forms of debt for certain reasons is a terrible idea, for example paying for luxuries such as a meal out or designer clothes you don't really need on a credit card. There's a reason why, after the initial buzz of the purchase, you often feel bad and negative: it's a huge mistake. Avoid getting into this kind of unnecessary debt at all costs.

You may be amazed to learn, therefore, that debt can be a great tool for significantly increasing our wealth. The key is controlling our emotions around debt and understanding how to use it effectively, rather than it using us.

If debt makes you feel 'yuck' and conjures up negative emotions, but in some cases can be helpful to you, how do you deal with this conflict? How do you find the debt 'sweet spot' for yourself? It's an important thing for you to consider and answer, and this chapter aims to solve much of it for you. The only missing pieces for you to factor in will be your own circumstances and risk tolerance to find the debt types and amounts that serve you, rather than you serving debt.

The bad, the ugly and the good

You may have heard of the movie *The Good, the Bad and the Ugly*, a spaghetti western starring Clint Eastwood. It is the final instalment in a trilogy of films, the first and second being *A Fistful of Dollars* and *A Few Dollars More*. It is apt that when I started to think about writing a chapter on debt, the first thought that came into my mind was the fact that it can be good, bad or ugly.

What is bad debt?

General examples of bad debt are:

- Debt incurred to purchase depreciating assets like a car.

- Debt incurred for lifestyle items like a holiday or clothing.

- Debt that has no tax benefits, ie we can't claim the costs of the debt itself, such as interest on the borrowing, as a tax deduction and/or we can't claim a tax deduction on the costs associated with the item we purchased. In most cases, a mortgage on our principal place of residence fits in this category so, to many people's surprise, a home loan is still considered a 'bad' debt.

- Credit cards or other high-interest debts of any type are bad simply by virtue of how much we incur in the way of extra costs on the borrowings if we don't pay them back on time.

What do you do with bad debt? Simple: avoid it wherever possible. If you do for some reason end up with bad debt, pay it off as quickly as possible and focus instead on good debt.

What is ugly debt?

Ugly debt is not a common financial term like good and bad debt. I have made it up. It is the one we can feel in our chest and hear in our mind. It's the one that keeps us awake at night because we have gone in above our head and overcommitted ourselves with how much we have borrowed. It is when the structure or potential impacts of the debt position are at a level that is not appropriate. We are exposed to too much risk and it is affecting our happiness and ability to function, as well as jeopardising our financial security. For some, the old saying of 'bite off more than you can chew and chew like crazy' is an effective approach to things, but for most of us, if we are feeling significant stress, worry and even fear about our debts, we are in an ugly debt position.

Ugly debt could be good debt or bad debt. It's more the sheer volume of debt that makes it ugly, but of course, bad ugly debt is worse than good ugly debt.

MY UGLY DEBT

I had ugly debt as a result of my divorce. As part of my divorce settlement I agreed to take on all the debt of the relationship. Given I had bought a business and a house not long prior, I already had a lot of debt, and divorce meant I was now also in a one-income household. In addition, I had significant child support obligations.

All these things combined meant I had a large amount of debt and I was stressed about it. I thought about it a lot, it was freaking me out and I didn't feel comfortable. If certain things didn't go well, then it could create financial problems for me. This is a classic example of ugly debt.

Not enjoying being in an ugly debt position, I knew I had to reduce some risk and stress. I didn't want to sell my business, so the obvious solution was to sell the property I had just bought before my marriage ended. I had some local agents come out and appraise it and discuss it.

During that process, one agent mentioned he had a client looking to rent a property for their employees as they had just won a big contract with the local council and the work would take about eight months. He advised me what the property could rent out for and his fees, and I calculated that the rent would meet the loan repayments on the house. My business income could then service the other debts.

I didn't want to sell the house as I absolutely loved it. I've also always been a believer in not making rash or big decisions during times of heightened stress or significant life events, so I agreed to rent it out. This instantly eased some of the pressures of the overall debt repayments and gave me time to adjust to my new life and financial circumstances.

My overall level of debt was still ugly because, although the rental income was helping to service the debt, it wasn't going to make a huge impact on the actual balance owing. What I had done, though, was buy myself some time and a little bit of breathing space to feel less stressed about it all.

As each month went on, my mind got clearer about a whole bunch of things. With greater clarity and calmness and seeing some small progress in getting the loan balances down a little, I was in a position after the eight-month tenant agreement to make a more measured assessment of what I would do. By that time, another opportunity had arisen: to use the property regularly as an Airbnb.

I liked the idea that the rental income could assist with reducing the loan against the property, while I could enjoy it for holidays as well. This helped me to see a potential range of lifestyle and financial payoffs, two of the big elements of the SELF Method.

In my case, time allowed an ugly debt to become more comfortable. Another thing on my side was the fact that although it was an ugly debt, the majority of it was good debt, not bad debt, as it related to a property that was producing income and has expenses so I could claim the loan costs as a tax deduction. That was an important factor in me being willing to ride it out instead of rushing for the sell button.

I tell you what, though, being in ugly debt is not fun. Avoid it if you can, preferably by not getting yourself in that situation in the first place. Of course, big events like divorce or an unexpected business failure can mean ugly debt is taken out of your control, but if possible, don't over commit yourself. The risks and stresses of ugly debt are not worth it.

What is good debt?

As the name suggests, if you are going to have debt, this is the type you want. Good debt is tax deductible. In other words, all the interest you pay the bank or lender, you can claim back against the tax you pay. In addition, other costs associated with the property you have invested in through the use of the borrowed funds are tax deductible. For example, if you bought an investment property, you can claim the rates and insurance and other property costs as a tax deduction. If you have bought shares, you can claim any broker-age or portfolio fees as a tax deduction. Many people don't know you can borrow to invest in shares; they think that property is the only option.

Tax deductibility is the main reason people refer to this type of debt as 'good', but the other key factor is good debt is usually incurred for investment purposes. If it wasn't, then the tax deduction wouldn't apply. Rather than borrowing to buy cars or clothes, you use the money you borrow to invest in something with the aim of gen-erating higher returns than the cost of the borrowings. In this way, good debt creates good financial outcomes.

How can good debt help you grow wealth?

While the tax benefits are nice and certainly helpful, the main reason good debt can help you grow your wealth is because it can potentially magnify your gains. Essentially, it allows you to use someone else's money as a capital base for investment. If what you have invested in achieves positive returns, you generate those returns on a high sum of money far sooner and probably at a greater scale than if you'd waited until you had saved up, meaning you are creating the potential to grow your wealth more rapidly. Using borrowed funds to invest is often referred to as gearing.

It is important to point out that if good debt can magnify your gains, it can also magnify your losses. If the investments you purchase do not perform well and go down in value, you will incur losses not only on your own funds invested, but also on the borrowed funds. At the same time, you will still be liable to pay back the original loan.

This is the risk of borrowing to invest, so if you are going to follow this route, make sure you have assessed your overall position. What is an appropriate amount of debt? What type of investments are you going to purchase? Other factors, such as having a stable income, ability to make debt repayments, insurances and investing for the right timeframes, are also critical for risk mitigation.

Consider what you will use as security and the type of loan you will take out. Typically, the investment itself is the security, and either an investment loan against an investment property or a margin loan against shares is the approach. Make yourself aware of how these loan structures work and the risks associated with them before jumping into any form of gearing. They will vary depending on the loans and investments used, so be sure to seek the help of a professional financial advisor.

Done well, good debt can be an effective way to invest, particularly when interest rates are low so the returns you'll require to outperform the cost of borrowing are equally low.

Debt as a motivator

Ugly debt is unenjoyable and scary. That is 100% true, but the right amount of 'fear' in life is often one of the biggest drivers of high performance. Some of the most successful people in history have spoken about their fear of failure as being key to their achievements. Others have spoken about their circumstances meaning that they simply had no option but to find a way to the other side through sheer determination and hard work.

In the context of business, many entrepreneurs started out with nothing and had many failures along the way, but they continued on towards their eventual success. For that, they must have had strong motivation, which may well initially have come from the risks associated with ugly debt.

Getting ourselves out of our comfort zone and having an appropriate level of fear in our lives can be a great way to motivate us to work harder, perform better and push for bigger results than we would if we were all warm and fuzzy and comfortable. Debt can induce that fear in us. It can be a motivator; it can be the thing that necessitates greater effort, getting us out of bed early on cold mornings. It might change our spending or saving decisions to ensure better financial habits. It might give us accountability because we know we must meet our repayment obligations. In this way, even ugly debt can be positive from the perspective of growing wealth.

MY MOTIVATIONAL MORTGAGE

When I bought my first property, I proudly went into my boss's office to tell him what I had done over the weekend. He was genuinely happy for me and gave me wholehearted congratulations.

It's what he said next that I didn't expect. 'We love our employees having debt, Josh,' he told me. 'It's a great reason for them to work harder so they can pay their mortgage.' I had a great relationship with him, so I in no way took this as offensive or rude, but it made me realise I had never thought about debt as a motivator until that time.

Since then, I have taken on debt for numerous reasons: other property purchases; investments; buying into my business. Over time, with the experience of using debt for various purposes – growing wealth and, at times, for lifestyle (buying homes only, not cars or clothes) – I can completely see how debt has acted as a great form of motivation for me to keep striving and keep going. In the main because I had to.

Debt and the associated obligations mean that if you want to keep what you have and push for more, you have to get up and work for it. Having experienced both high and low levels of debt, I can 100% guarantee that during the periods of little debt and full comfort from a financial perspective, I have not had as high a level of drive or reason to push harder.

Personally, I like what debt can do. The way it can assist us with growing our wealth and enhancing our lifestyle is great, as long as we don't get ourselves in too deep.

Summary

Debt, along with the sets of emotions it can put upon us, is often confusing. In this chapter, we have clarified the different types of debt and seen how we can use it for both financial gain and motivation.

To summarise, we need to:

- Aim for good debt; avoid bad and ugly debt

- Only use debt to invest after assessing our situation in detail to be aware of the risks

- Not think of debt as a completely bad thing

- Be aware that using debt to invest can be an effective tool in growing wealth

- Consider debt as a form of motivation to help us push harder and achieve more

- Ensure we have our debt structured correctly and get the best loan products in terms of interest rates, features, fees and requirements

Seeking guidance from a mortgage broker is a great way to get help with choosing the right loan products for your situation. Ideally any big investment or loan decisions should involve all your professional advisors such as accountant, financial advisor, mortgage broker and lawyer.

As always, we must do what is right for us as individuals and part of a family. An easily stressed low-risk taker won't want to take on debt as it is so far out of their comfort zone, while someone who is comfortable taking on risk and managing the emotions that come with it can use good debt wisely to achieve their goals.

PART FOUR
THE SELF METHOD – LIFESTYLE

Businesswoman and talk-show host Oprah Winfrey famously said, 'You can have it all, just not all at once.' For someone as wealthy and successful as Oprah to say that is powerful and sends out a really good and wise message. For most of us, who don't have infinite time or money available, it is 100% true. We can have all the things we want in our life, but it's difficult to obtain them all at once. It's a process, an evolution.

When it comes to living our best life, it's vital that we appreciate the fact it is a journey rather than focusing purely on the destination. Life, like investing, is not one perfect upwards trajectory without any bumps or adversities to overcome. We need to learn to appreciate some of the harder moments. Whether it be an ongoing challenge or just a small part of a day like a difficult meeting or frustrating event, we need to recognise that is life. It's normal.

While setbacks and annoyances are a natural part of life and we shouldn't expect pure blue sky and sunshine 24/7, there is nothing wrong with making every effort to have the things that we enjoy most as often as possible. There are some effective ways to maximise these things. Ironically enough, the secret to achieving this is similar to Oprah's quote. Similar, but not the same.

Read on to find out what I mean.

7
The 4Hs – Home, Holidays, Hobbies, Happy-hour

I am a big fan of saying, 'Ahhh, this is the life.' You know, the feeling you get when things are just good. You're happy, content, warm inside, calm in the mind and at ease and peace.

Sometimes it's a brief moment that causes this feeling and other times it's a whole event or experience. Sometimes it's a material thing, such as a new car or an expensive watch that you've been saving up for. Maybe it's a spa day, a night in a luxury hotel room or perhaps going to a 'premium' sporting event where you and your friends enjoy nice food, drinks and a lot of laughs while watching your favourite team take the win. Other times it might be a natural wonder like watching the sun set, the waves crash in or seeing a wild animal in its natural habitat. Maybe it's as simple as sinking down into your comfy chair to drink a cup of tea or read a book, or snuggling up next to your family on the couch for your favourite TV show.

On a larger scale, it could be admiring your newly finished home renovation, looking at it with pride and joy and having a little smile to yourself. Maybe you finally got to take that dream trip of a lifetime and it's everything you could have imagined and more. The sights, the sounds, the food, the culture – it all just makes you feel amazing and happy and on cloud nine.

It doesn't matter what gives you the 'Ahhh, this is the life' feeling, it's what I call 'lifestyle'. It will be different for all of us and that's what's awesome about it. What we want, feel and enjoy as lifestyle is unique to us. For some it requires a lot of money, for others it doesn't.

Personally, I'm pretty diverse. I love sitting by a campfire and enjoying the stars and moon overhead, really being at one with nature. I can also appreciate a beautiful hotel suite and going downstairs to an amazing breakfast on offer in the morning, then off to the gym and pool. I love a full-on day at football with my mates, cheering and screaming and willing my team on, just as much as I enjoy a relaxing cup of tea at home with my partner.

A recent material lifestyle item for me has been getting our house painted, replacing our oven and all the lighting throughout our house. I absolutely love our new lights and enjoying the huge difference they have made to the look of the rooms.

These are all examples of lifestyle for me. Lifestyle can be broad and that is a great thing, but some of our lifestyle desires will cost money. Sometimes a lot of money, so it's important we work out how best to enjoy as many of the lifestyle things we love as possible, while keeping our other needs on track.

Having asked hundreds of people about what's important to them from a lifestyle perspective, I have broadly categorised the most common responses that appear to bring the best outcomes into a lifestyle model. There are 4Hs in the lifestyle model, so an easy way to remember this is L4H.

The L4Hs are:

- Home

- Holidays

- Hobbies

- Happy-hour

Let's look at each one and explore how to get that 'Ahhh, this is the life' feeling as much as possible.

Home

Our homes are our havens. Home is a place where we can be ourselves and do what we want without the world watching or judging or being involved. We can make our homes look, feel and function how we want so we enjoy them and our time there as much as possible.

We don't have to own our home to achieve this. I know many people who can afford to own their home financially, but they prefer not to. Regardless of whether we own or rent, if it feels homely and comfortable, then we can enjoy many 'Ahh, this is the life' moments within our home.

What do you love about your current home? What would you want in a future home? For me, it's starting the day on the deck with the birds chirping and the sun breaking through the clouds as my partner and I sip our favourite tea or coffee. A barbecue outside on a warm summer's night; a movie night in winter with the family in the cosy lounge room. Or sitting by our open fire with a nice glass of wine. It's also nice to cook up a feast in a beautiful kitchen. While I'm not a great cook, my partner is, so that is next on our list: updating our kitchen. What would you like to change or improve about your home, or is it already everything you want?

We create a lot of happy memories in our home, but it is also a key part of us feeling safe and secure, having a sanctuary that we can retreat to when we just want to be 'us'. When we want to feel at ease and at peace in a space that we love and enjoy. This is why the home is without doubt one of the key parts of the L4H model. In fact, I find it is the lifestyle item people will usually invest the most money into, whether that be the purchase of the home or through the payment of rent. It simply costs a lot to put a roof over our heads and, in most cases, make it look and feel the way we want. We tend to be willing to contribute a reasonable portion of our income or funds to achieving that outcome because we spend a lot of time in our home.

Holidays

The ability to get out of the same surroundings, enjoy some variety and not feel we're stuck in Groundhog Day. That's what a holiday gives us. It's a chance to step off the day-to-day merry-go-round and stop being the juggling tightrope walker.

Holidays give us new experiences, new sights, new energy. They're a chance to recharge, refresh and reconnect. My family and I are excited to have booked two breaks in the coming months: one is a weekend away with some other families to stay near a beautiful beach along the stunning and world-famous Great Ocean Road. If you haven't been, check it out if you can. Hundreds of kilometres of amazing coastline and scenery with idyllic towns dotted along the journey. Six weeks later, we will be going to the beach to enjoy the summer weather. Surfing, swimming in the pool, jumping off the pier, long nature walks, sliding down the sand hill, a bit of fishing and definitely some beach sports and cold beers. Taking the days slowly, finding time to wind down and catch plenty of the 'Ahh, this is the life' vibes.

The beautiful thing about holidays is how they form part of our lifestyle. They could be as simple as a short drive to the nearby coast where most of the joys are free. The beach is a treasure chest of diverse things to do. They could involve a fifteen-hour flight over thousands of miles to explore a completely different continent and culture. What you and your family love in a holiday might be different to what my family loves, but we all still use this single word to describe it.

Holidays are without a doubt among the most sought-after and loved lifestyle items. Our desire for them lasts our entire lifetime. I have been lucky enough to travel to over thirty countries and experience some amazing things in the places I have visited, including a near-death experience bungee jumping over a fearsome rocky canyon in Ecuador, but I have so much more I want to do and explore with my family. I bet you do too.

In Chapter 3, when we looked at steering our wealth machine, I highly recommended paying regular amounts into a savings account set aside exclusively for holidays. This ensures we have money available for them so we can book, plan and pay for them in advance and enjoy the lead up, not just the actual holiday. Financially, this works well as it gives us a set amount to use for holidays each year and we can plan on that basis. We don't end up spending more than we can afford or putting a holiday on credit and creating a financial headache that spoils the memories once we get home.

How much are you going to put towards holidays each year? Where are you off to next?

Hobbies

What do you love doing? What are your passions? Are you an artistic and creative type? Do you love reading, films, theatre, opera, live music, concerts, festivals, dance, the arts?

Are sports your thing? Is it a team sport or an individual one? Is it high intensity with contact like football or basketball, or more skills-focused like golf or tennis?

What about cars or motor sports, or extreme sports like dirt bikes, BMX, skating? Are you into endurance events like long-distance cycling, swimming or running? Maybe you are into something more obscure or unique. Are you a watcher or a doer?

Regardless of your answers to all these questions, I can almost guarantee that as a busy working parent, you will have a long list of things you used to love that you no longer do. Why? It's generally because of a lack of time and increased work and family commitments, coupled with age and energy levels and money being directed elsewhere. These all mean it's hard to keep your hobbies and passions in your life.

I challenge you to change that right now. Write down a list of all the things you used to do that would fit in the broad category of hobbies. Just get them all down on paper. If you're in a relationship, ask your partner to make a list of their own.

With your list complete, put a line through any that don't interest you much anymore. Now put a line through any that aren't practical anymore. For example, at age thirty-nine, I realised quite a long time ago that there is little to be gained from me playing full-contact Aussie-rules football again. The last thing I need is a broken leg so I can't properly look after my kids, but the non-contact version of Aussie rules is a great alternative. It's fun and I can play it, so I do.

What's on your list? What could you get back into enjoying again, either as a spectator or actually doing? Could you join a painting class, learn to play a musical instrument or take up a creative pursuit? Would joining the local sports team or club get you back out there, keep it fun and make you accountable to carry on?

It's so important to set aside time for our hobbies and passions. They are a key part of our lifestyle and enjoyment of life. They can also create a sense of freedom and individuality and give us our identity away from being mum or dad or our job title.

Hobbies do, of course, come at a cost, so ensure you set money aside for the things you enjoy as part of your financial plan. I'm sure you will love having them back in your life, even if they're modified versions, and that they will be a huge contributor to your lifestyle.

One that I gave up many years ago was playing the drums, but just this month I purchased a drum kit and it's been amazing getting back into it.

I challenge you to get back into yours and bring those passions back into your life.

Happy-hour

When I hear the words 'happy-hour', I envisage ice-cold drinks, relaxing afternoons and fun with friends at a pub or the hotel bar. Better still, the hotel swim-up bar – what an amazing invention they are.

What do you picture? Even if you don't drink, you might think of a delicious mocktail or hanging out with friends and seeing everyone relaxed and happy. Perhaps you see time with no kids around, either on a getaway on your own, a night out, or just a few hours off from parenting duties when they've gone to their grandparents' or friend's house. Whatever thoughts and feelings the words 'happy-hour' conjure up for you, there is no doubt it is the global statement for fun, relaxation and, as the name suggests, feeling happy. I encourage you to create regular happy-hour-style events in your life.

Deliberately plan for things to be fully funded as part of your finances to give you ongoing happy-hour moments. Put them in the calendar in advance so you have something to look forward to, and then you get the light and shade of different things happening. Mini celebrations dotted throughout your month to help break up the normal routine. They add excitement and spark to your life. It's not just the actual moment that is enjoyable, but also the anticipation and memories of it.

Here are some things that can go on your happy-hour event list:

- **A regular date night.** If you're in a relationship, set an hour or two aside each week to create something fun and unique together. If going out is difficult, then you can still have a date night at home.

- **A family-based happy-hour.** Maybe set a night where you get take-out of everyone's favourite food and drinks and have a great time sharing stories of the week and enjoying a few laughs. You don't have to cook, so that's one less job to do. The devices go away and you all engage.

- **The 'real' happy-hour at a cocktail bar or the hotel swim-up bar.** This is the ultimate experience, but it's not always possible. Enjoy these elite versions of happy-hour when you can, but find ways to create and build into your routine more regular happy-hour events. They will make a huge difference to how you feel, boosting your lifestyle and enjoyment of life.

A little lifestyle tip

Earlier I spoke about RAKs. My tweak on that is random acts of cash (RACs). Keep a little aside in your fun accounts (explained in Chapter 3) to use for RACs. It doesn't need to be a large amount you choose, $20–$50 per week is fine. Then use this money to practise RACs in addition to everything you already do to provide for the family. Unexpectedly buy them something nice. On a boring afternoon, suddenly jump up with excitement and exclaim to everyone, 'LET'S GET ICE-CREAM!'

These little unexpected treats – they're not big amounts or lavish gifts – can bring regular boosts of energy and excitement to your lifestyle. You will feel great, and so will your family members receiving them.

Summary

Lifestyle is so important for all of us. There's no point living a life that is dull and boring and not giving us what we want. The L4H model works really well for people; I have seen it. It gives them the lifestyle items that they truly desire.

The L4Hs – home, holidays, hobbies and happy-hour – cover big things, little things, regular things and irregular things. There are things for individuals, couples and the whole family. They tick all the boxes as they are as broad and diverse as we are. Your L4Hs are whatever suits you as the categories don't contain anything specific. You can make your home, holiday, hobby and happy-hour whatever you want it to be.

The L4Hs do come at a cost, so we need to make sure we strike the balance of enjoying our lifestyle items while achieving our financial and wealth goals. The key to doing this is not wasting money on lifestyle items that aren't of high importance or high value to us. We can't have or do every single thing, so we need to focus on the ones that matter most to us and give us the highest payoff.

Oprah said, 'You can have it all, just not all at once.' I would encourage you to think about a great lifestyle from the perspective of, 'You don't *need* it all.' Eradicate things that cost you money, time or energy if they are not giving you a high-lifestyle payoff. You can then direct more valuable resources to the ones that really are.

8

The Pool, The Private School, The Porsche

One part of the Parental Balance Model is the tight-rope between lifestyle goals and financial goals.

Lifestyle Goals		Financial Goals

In Chapter 7, I outlined my L4H model. If people are meeting and engaging in these 4Hs on a regular basis, in my experience, they are generally happy with their lifestyle.

However, sometimes big-ticket items come along: life-style decisions and choices that cost a lot. They may or may not turn out to mean a lot to us (sometimes in hindsight, we realise they don't), but they feel impor-tant to us at the time of the decision and can mess with our head. Should we or shouldn't we? Do we need it or just want it? Are we getting the two confused? Do we not really care, but the kids are dying for it? I'm sure you can see how these ones get tricky. Believe me, choices like this will come up in your life on a fairly regular basis.

To illustrate big lifestyle choices, let's look at three examples called the 3Ps – the pool, the private school and the Porsche.

The pool

Personally, I absolutely love pools. I was lucky enough to grow up with two pools as my parents got divorced when I was about six and for the majority of my life, they both lived in houses with a pool. Not crazy, fancy tailor-made concrete pools that cost six figures; some were above ground and relatively basic, but they were big and fun and got constant use, especially from me. Given I grew up in a town that's consistently above 40 degrees Celsius in summer, they were pretty much a necessity, too.

I still remember one day standing up on the side of my mum's pool ladder, announcing to the world that I was about to do the biggest bomb in history and getting ready for a world-shaking cannonball. If you have seen the movie *Anchorman*, you will recall Will Ferrell proudly crashing down into the pool in all his glory. That was me, but a seven-year-old version, talking it up big time, when suddenly out of nowhere, bang! Right on my butt, I got stung by a bee.

At that stage of my life, I was allergic to bees and they scared the hell out of me. That sure slowed me down and sent me from planned cannonball to cannoning into mum's arms as I swelled up and welled up all at once. Thankfully, all my other memories spent in pools are happy ones.

Even though we lived close to a river, a pool was still without doubt money well spent. For the amount of entertainment and lifestyle enjoyment it provided, it was pretty much a no brainer from a financial perspective. Also, as it was so hot where we lived, a pool was often a requirement when anyone came to sell their home, so it would deliver a financial return too.

That said, spending money on a pool is not always a simple decision. I have discussed the topic of putting a pool in my current home with my partner and the kids. As a pool lover, I am open to it, but my financial mind says no for a number of reasons. I will share my reasoning to give you an example of the amount of considerations you need to take into account and angles you need to look at when making any big lifestyle decision. This is where that handy little ELF comes into its own again.

Melbourne's climate is quite a lot cooler than where I grew up. There are about four months of genuine swimming weather and maybe five to six months where the more brave and keen swimmers would get in the pool if it was heated. We also live close to the beach, which is easy to access and enjoy during the four warm months.

Melbourne is one of the most expensive property markets in the world. Thankfully, we do have a decent-size back yard and can fit in a pool if we want to, but is that the best use of our space? If we came to sell, many people in Melbourne wouldn't see a pool as an attractive feature as they wouldn't need it or use it enough. A pool may improve the value of property in some places, but in others, it can reduce the number of potential buyers as people don't want the cost and effort required to maintain and clean it.

What do I do in this case? What would you do? You will face similar conundrums. How can you get from confusion to clarity when making a decision like this? How can you be confident you have made the right decision and are directing your resources to the highest payoff areas?

Re-enter your helpful ELF. When decisions and choices like this arise, sit down with your family (if the kids are old enough) and analyse the different components of the emotional, lifestyle and financial parts of the SELF Method.

In the case of my pool conundrum, this is how it turned out for my partner and me.

Emotional:

- The four kids will love it.

- We will create a lot of great memories as a family.

- We get strong positive emotions when we think about having a pool.

- It will improve the look, feel and enjoyment of our home. Even when it's not in use, it will be a nice addition to our yard.

That is a big 'yes' for the pool from an emotional perspective from all family members.

Lifestyle:

- It's a great way to entertain and reason to have friends over.

- I grew up loving having a pool and the lifestyle it gave me. I know my kids will love it too, even if the relatively cool weather and the beach nearby means there is less need for a pool in Melbourne than in my hometown.

- It gives an extra reason for the kids to spend time with us and each other at home. We love our time with them as a family, so that's a big lifestyle plus.

- It's not just about swimming; from a lifestyle perspective, sitting by the pool with a book, favourite drink or some music provides a calming feeling.

I'd estimate my partner will get in the pool about three times per year, yet she is keen to get one so she can enjoy being near it. I will probably get in it about fifty times a year, yet I'm less certain. The kids are becoming excited – the pool seems to be getting the lifestyle tick.

Financial:

- Some people say a pool is a terrible financial decision: the upfront cost, the ongoing maintenance etc. As a financial advisor, I can agree with a lot of this.

- A decent-looking in-ground pool is not cheap. We need to be able to afford it without it impacting other parts of our lifestyle or financial goals too much.

- In many cases, a nicely designed pool can attract buyers of the right demographic when we come to sell, especially as we will have sufficient remaining yard space for other things. While a pool may reduce the number of potential buyers, it could attract the interest of the right buyers.

Before we went through the process properly (using the ELF approach), my mind was turning to the upfront cost and the potential impact on the future saleability of our home. The financial factors were holding me back, especially once I thought about the true level of use the pool might get.

Once we considered all factors and I allowed the broader considerations of the ELF into the decision, I started to see things differently. It was only then that I thought about my childhood spent swimming all day and into the evening. I thought about when we are on holiday somewhere with a pool, how much the kids love it and spend all day in there. In our case, the emotional and lifestyle elements of this decision were so strongly in favour that the financial reasons to say no needed to be much greater than I had realised.

In addition, while the upfront and ongoing costs are a key factor, my fears about the future value or saleability of our house were allayed when I realised that many other young families would be attracted to the same emotional and lifestyle factors that are in favour of the pool. As you can probably guess by now, we will be getting a pool.

You can use this approach with similar lifestyle choices for your family, noting they are choices, not necessities. That's what can make them hard, but the ELF approach allows you to factor in all the key elements of the decision and ensure you are going to get an appropriate payoff across your emotional, lifestyle and financial areas.

The private school

The terminology can vary in different countries, but in Australia, a public school is a government school where what you pay out of your own pocket for your kids to attend is less than it is for a private school, which comes at a substantial cost in terms of what you must pay directly yourself. The larger and more prestigious private schools in Australia come at a cost of around $35,000 per student per year, and these fees generally rise by about 6% every year. Depending on whether your children attend from primary school or secondary school and how many children you have, that means there is the potential for private school fees to be over $1 million for some families. If that's not a big financial decision, then I don't know what is.

For some, the cost is not an issue; they have the financial resources to pay and are certain that private schooling is the best option for their kids. Some can afford it, but prefer to send their kids to a public school. For others, the cost makes the decision for them. They simply can't afford private education so their kids go to a public school. There are those who can't afford it themselves, but they want their kids to go to a private school and are lucky to have parents or grandparents in a strong enough financial position to pay the school fees. Finally, there are people who can do it at a stretch. It's possible, but the financial factor is a large consideration and it would mean a lot of planning and sacrificing other things.

What do you do? You may want to make it happen, but the financial cost of sending your kids to private school is significant enough that it's not simply a matter of ticking the box and paying the fees each month.

Let's welcome back the ELF.

Emotional:

- Weigh up the emotions and reasons behind why you'd prefer your kids to attend a private school rather than a public school.

- What about the emotions of the child themselves? While this is predominantly a decision for the parents, could a long commute or none of their friends going to the same school have a big negative impact on them?

- Would the stress of the cost of private schooling have a serious impact on the important 4Hs of the emotional model in your life?

- What emotions and visions and mental images do you conjure up when you picture the kids at a public school and at a private school?

Lifestyle:

- Would having your children at a certain school improve or detract from your lifestyle overall?

- Would it improve their lifestyle or detract from it?

- What sort of school suits them, their personality, their hobbies, their areas of talent and interest? What is the best style and type of education for them?

- If the cost is a big factor for you, would paying for private schooling substantially reduce your ability to enjoy the 4Hs of the lifestyle model?

Financial:

If you can easily afford private school, or your parents or grandparents can and are willing to pay, this is a simple decision, but if the financial element is a factor:

- Have you truly assessed the total cost? Not just the fees, but all the additional costs that can come with private schooling.

- Have you projected out the cost, factoring in the number of years of schooling and the number of children you have and the fact that private school fees often go up faster than other living expenses?

- Have you considered the further costs if your children attend university?

- Have you looked at an ongoing savings and investment plan or tax-effective ways to invest that can make it easier for you to meet these ongoing costs?

Using the ELF allows us to take a calculated and methodical approach to a large decision. Private schooling is not a necessity, it is a lifestyle choice. Understandably, it is an important one, because we all want the best for our kids and that includes an excellent education, but if there will be financial pressures and stresses as a result of such a decision, it is vital that we plan and allow for them. We don't want meeting one part of our plans to derail a whole bunch of other parts of the SELF Method. That's when we will get off balance and things will go pear shaped. Problems, stresses, unhappiness and other issues can then arise, and cracks can appear and be hard to repair.

Private schooling is a useful example to include in the 3Ps. Public schooling is an option and Australia (along with many other countries) has excellent schools, both public and private. It's just some people prefer the idea of private school.

The Porsche

Some classic cars could be viewed as an investment as they go up significantly in value, but cars are generally one of the worst investment decisions you can make from a financial viewpoint. Especially brand-new luxury cars. They have high upfront costs; they depreciate in value quickly; they have significant ongoing fees via insurances, maintenance and repairs. In other words, they are purely an expense, not an investment.

Many of you probably already know this, but if you don't, then please read the previous paragraph a few times. Get clear in your mind that buying a brand-new luxury car is about the worst financial decision you can make.

For some people, this knowledge will not make an ounce of difference. They don't know cars, they don't particularly like cars, they don't care about cars. A car is just a thing that gets them where they need to go and they're not worried what make, model or year it is. They aren't fussed by how it looks, as long as it works.

Other people love cars and know everything about them. They are interested in the history, the brands, the models, how they work. They may even have some skills with car mechanics, a passion for doing up cars or racing them or belonging to a car club.

Others love everything about cars, inside and out. How they feel, how they run and how it makes them feel to drive a certain car or be seen in a certain car. Beyond putting fuel in and turning the car on, they may know little about them, but they love the feelings that come from having a certain car. If they don't have it, they have strong feelings about wanting it.

What do people who love nice cars do when they are such a bad financial choice? When it is an absolute no brainer that the financial impacts of spending money on cars amount to a really bad decision? Let's look at some real-life examples of how different people approached this decision. All the names are made up.

LET'S GO FOR A SPIN

Brian loves cars and knows a lot about them. He races them, can fix them and even knows how to make parts for them. He is car savvy, recognising what they are worth so he can find and negotiate a bargain.

He is also smart with his money and in a good financial position. The combination of not overspending on his lifestyle passion while putting aside the finances to engage in it means that Brian finds a perfect balance of enjoying cars, ticking off all his emotional desires and not putting pressure on his family's financial position.

Anne has owned multiple extremely expensive cars, some of the most prestigious and beautiful machines ever made, and loves driving them. She is not necessarily hugely knowledgeable or interested in cars in the way that Brian is, but her emotional attachment to them is strong. Anne is a successful businesswoman and has an excellent income, so she can afford the cars, but there is no doubt that her level of financial wealth would be much higher if she had not chosen to spend so much money on luxury vehicles.

In terms of her ELF, Anne ticks her emotional and lifestyle boxes by having nice cars, but has negatively impacted her financial outcomes. Due to her resources, this has not led to financial issues or stresses for herself or her family. They have still been able to live a good life and do the other things they want to.

Peter and his partner have two nice cars as their daily drives. Nothing crazy, but perfectly respectable 'mid-range' cars. They do not need another car, but Peter has always wanted a Porsche. He has a good job and a healthy income and a strong asset base, but he also has a reasonable level of debt against those assets and a large portion of it is bad debt.

Paying down this debt would be a wise financial decision, but Peter is young and wants to enjoy his life. He also wants to make wise financial decisions; he is intelligent and understands money and the cost of buying an expensive car he doesn't need. In addition, he is not a showy or materialistic person. He doesn't want the Porsche to drive it around in front of everyone; he just really likes this make of car and wants one for himself.

In the end, Peter's emotional drivers outweighed the financial considerations and he bought a Porsche. He did a lot of research and found his preferred model, which certainly wasn't the cheapest Porsche to drive around. For that reason, he doesn't get to use it a lot, but he does enjoy it.

Paul is worth millions. He has been extremely successful in business, but doesn't own a car at all. He just catches an Uber if he needs to. Given that the annual cost of using Uber could in many cases be less than the cost of car insurance, servicing and maintenance, maybe Paul is on to something.

With total wealth of around $50 million, Kate lives in a nice home, but nothing extravagant. She drives a Nissan and her husband drives a Honda as they prefer to give to their family, community and charities. She is a generous person, so it's giving and seeing the benefits that she brings to the lifestyles of others that ticks her emotional boxes. Material possessions, including fancy cars, don't feature highly in her ELF considerations.

What do we do when we are faced with a decision like this? We really want that top-of-the-range car, but we know it's an extravagance and a first-world problem. It's not even a lifestyle item like an ordinary car; it's a luxury purchase with zero financial reasoning or value to it.

The ELF fits this situation too, but tread carefully and spend extra time pondering a decision like this. If the financial outcome is obviously negative and the car will only add to your emotional or lifestyle outcomes, it's important not to rush and go overboard. The emotional and lifestyle benefits of a Porsche (or whatever the make might be) can rapidly wear off when the negative impacts on your financial wealth are too high. It might feel highly desirable when you are considering it, but the true value it adds to your and your family's life overall may not be that significant.

Just as money won't make you happy, it simply helps to enhance an already happy life, so it is with the Porsche. It may make you feel momentarily happy to drive it from the showroom, but at what cost to your other emotional, lifestyle and financial goals? If you really love cars and you can afford a luxury model without it having a detrimental impact on too many other areas, then go for it. If you can't, then don't.

Summary

This book is not about guiding you to the most boring and basic life possible. Quite the opposite, in fact. I want you to be inspired and motivated to achieve the best lifestyle possible as a result of managing your finances more effectively, but when it comes to any big lifestyle expense, make sure you really take your time to assess the potential ELF payoff.

It is also vital to assess the true financial cost. For example, a luxury car might cost $100,000, but in twenty years be worth a mere $5,000. If invested well, that $100,000 you used to purchase it could be worth many hundreds of thousands in twenty years. What are you truly sacrificing to have that item? Significant wealth? Future financial freedom? A passive income stream which could create an ongoing dream lifestyle?

Philosopher Bertrand Russell said, 'It is preoccupation with possessions, more than anything else, that prevents us from living freely and nobly.' This quote gives some perspective to the potential improvement to our lives that material items will bring. Will too many material things have a detrimental impact on our lives and lifestyle? Will too much time, energy or money spent on 'stuff' actually weigh us down and hold us back, rather than make our lives more fulfilling?

Only you can determine what is right for you and your life, but tread carefully with large lifestyle purchases and expenditures. Be 100% certain you are making the right choice for enhancing your life and the lives of your family. A pool, private school and Porsche are just some of the many potential examples we may face, but this recommended approach will serve you well in all such instances.

9

Today Versus The Future

The short-term versus long-term tightrope on the Parental Balance Model is a highly strung and challenging one.

| Short-Term Goals | Long-Term Goals |

Things like distractions, emotions, keeping up with the Joneses and seeing all the beautiful possessions and experiences we want to be enjoying become hard to ignore at times. Understandably, we all want to live a great life in the here and now, especially in today's society where everything is so accessible at the click of a button or the tap of a card. We are faced with a dilemma because we see and want so much right now, but only have a certain amount of resources and years to work to build up assets for our whole lives. We may feel some obligation to ensure we are creating the future lifestyle we want, as well as guilt if we're not doing so.

This can create a range of emotions. A good way to describe it is that it's like having a split personality, each with its own name. First, we have Super Sammy Short-Term. Everyone loves Sammy: she's a fun girl, always up for adventures, holidays, socialising and living it up. Not a care in the world, happy go lucky, laughing, singing and doing what she likes.

Then there is Languishing Larry Long-Term. He is tired, flat, boring, stale and nowhere near as awesome as Sammy. He doesn't have the zest for life or spark that Sammy does.

When we get the sugar-hit rush of living and thinking like Sammy, we tend to feel good. Why wouldn't we? We are getting what we want when we want. Focusing on sensible old Larry does not give us good vibes and make us want to kick off our shoes and dance around the kitchen to our favourite song. I get it. It's hard to ignore Sammy and give a bit more love to Larry. It doesn't come naturally, but let's explore how we can think and act to see the appeal and benefit in both.

Short-term lifestyle

Particularly when kids are dependent on us (and often hard to say no to when they're wearing us down), the number of lifestyle goals and demands on a family can be huge. Not to mention our own short-term lifestyle goals and things we want in our lives. Because the current moment is directly in the vision of our wealth machine windscreen, we naturally focus more on the short term. It's right there in front of us, staring us down.

This is where the Parental Balance Model is of great use to us. It helps us stay upright on this particular tightrope so we don't topple over in any one area, in this case falling into the chasm of the short term. As always, striking a balance requires some compromise. Unless we have a bottomless pit of money, we simply cannot do every single thing we want right now.

Without unlimited resources, how do we feel content and satisfied with our short-term lifestyle? Here are a few tips:

- Get clear on what you truly want for your short-term lifestyle. By short-term, I refer to the period from today until three years into the future. Three to ten years is medium term and ten years plus is long term. What do you really want day-to-day over the next three years from a lifestyle perspective?

- Review what you have written and remove anything that isn't jumping out at you. If it isn't super exciting, then bin it.

- Remove any items you don't have to achieve or gain in the next three years, relocating them in a separate list for medium- to long-term lifestyle goals and items.

- Review the list again. As you are doing it, visualise the things you want in the long term. Is it early retirement, financial security, a certain amount of wealth or investments, greater freedom and flexibility? With your eye on your long-term prizes, edit your short-term list and see if you can direct more money and energy into the longer-term lifestyle goals you are picturing.

- Discuss your lists via a review with your family, if the kids are old enough, and/or your partner if you have one. Do this in a productive and constructive way, then make further amendments until you are set on what your true short-term lifestyle goals are.

For the majority of us, this process will get us to a balanced short-term lifestyle outcome. We will have enough things on our short-term list to keep Sammy excited, inspired and happy while bringing relief and security to our inner Larry as we are putting resources towards creating our best future life.

Long-term lifestyle

Did you go into detail when you visualised what you want long term? If not, do this now. Think, write, draw and search for ideas and images that best describe and embody the future lifestyle you want to lead. Building a vision board like I mentioned earlier is even better. Where are you? Who are you with? What are you wearing, eating, drinking, hearing?

Is it quiet or loud? Warm or cold? Local or overseas? Busy or slow paced? Similar to now or vastly different? What are you doing? What activities, groups, clubs, associations, friends and family are you picturing in your life? Are there kids and grandkids sprawled around, or are they far enough away that you can see them as much as you wish, but you aren't on full-time duties?

Is it an extravagant and expensive existence where you live by the motto, 'I can't take it with me, so I'm going to spend the kids' inheritance'? Or is it not about the expense but about the experience, and you feel you don't need a huge amount of money to live your dream future life?

When you are caught up in the now, it can be hard to picture the longer term, especially if the now is busy and you are jumping from one thing to the next. How can you think about ten years from now in detail when you are focusing on today's long list of to-do items?

Completing this exercise will help you to focus. Set aside time to go through this process, even for a short time to start with, for example, twenty minutes. You will find that once you get started, your thoughts will flow easily, and you will likely come up with a clear picture of what your ideal long-term lifestyle looks like. Keep working on it until it feels fairly accurate. Then use this as a base to evolve and edit over time as new feelings, thoughts and ideas come to mind.

Stick to the #makefinancesfun motto as you complete this, because creating and building your best long-term lifestyle should be a fun thing to do. This is one of the benefits of the process – enjoying beautiful mental images and thoughts of your amazing future life.

The other main purpose and benefit? Moving Larry from languishing to loved. When we are clear on how great our future can be and what we are striving towards, it's not a negative thing. It's not a sacrifice to take a bit from Sammy anymore because we can see the payoff from contributing to Larry and striking that balance.

By going through the steps above, you should be clear on the lifestyle you are wanting both short and long term. But how do you know if it is achievable and if you are going to hit those targets, especially when the long-term goals are so far away?

Re-enter our old friend the wealth machine. The various parts of the wealth machine described earlier will help you assess the affordability and estimated funding required to go towards your short- and long-term goals. In addition to this, I recommend doing some projections to work out your expected longer-term financial position if you take certain decisions and assume approximate levels of returns on your investments. You can also analyse the likely amount of funds required to meet your retirement objectives by factoring in your planned retirement age, life expectancies and how much you anticipate you will need to spend each year to enjoy your dream retirement. If you don't have the time, knowledge or software to do this, reach out to a professional financial advisor who can help.

Is it lifestyle or financial?

We have all done it. Convinced ourselves that something is a wise financial choice being done for a perceived financial benefit, when it is not. In such instances, the old saying of 'perception is reality' is true. We tell ourselves we are doing something because it will help us financially, but, in reality, we want to make ourselves feel better about spending on a lifestyle item.

The biggest example of this is our homes. We think a home is an investment that will always go up in value and give us financial security. Yes, many homes do go up in value, but are they the best financial use of our money, and do they really provide the best investment return? No, they don't for these reasons:

- Loans and other costs aren't tax deductible. This is bad debt.

- Generally, we do not generate an income-based return from them as we don't rent out our home. While Airbnb has changed this for some, usually there is minimal income return from our homes.

- Ongoing costs of rates, insurance, maintenance and improvements are significant.

- Many homes will see their capital value increase, but not all.

- We forget to factor in numerous items when looking at what we perceive as the financial result they created. We look at what we paid for it and what we sold it for, and in many cases that is a significantly greater figure, but we forget the upfront entry costs, the ongoing costs and the exit costs. Once these costs are factored in on top of the fact that we didn't generate any tax benefits or income benefits, we will see how our homes can actually generate poor total financial returns compared to other options.

For these reasons, I refer to a home as a lifestyle asset. Keep that in mind when considering your assets and financial and lifestyle decisions. There are many other examples of this, such as the pool I spoke about earlier. Will it add value to your home, or do you just want one? Thinking about cars, will that Porsche appreciate in value and be considered a collector's item, or does it just look awesome and is fun to drive?

There is absolutely nothing wrong with buying any lifestyle item you want. If it fits in with your plans and ticks enough of your ELF boxes, go and buy, and enjoy the things that matter to you. What is wrong is convincing yourself you are doing it for a financial reason if there is little evidence that the purchase will improve (or preferably maximise) your investment returns and financial position. Taking this approach will help you to recognise what and where you are allocating to lifestyle and likely prevent you from overbalancing in this area and ensure you are dedicating enough to the financial category for both the short and long term.

When people say to me, 'I don't know where the money goes, we don't live an extravagant lifestyle', there is usually more lifestyle going on than they might perceive or realise. It's relative in our minds, and until we get it clear in front of us via our structural and wealth machine tools and figures, we can't see the forest through the trees.

Sometimes only experience and hindsight will help us learn that we can get a lot of 'lifestyle' out of things already in our life. If not in our eyes, then at least in our children's eyes. A great example of this was when I took my son on a holiday.

Not long after my marriage separation, I attended a charity event dinner which included a fundraiser auction. I bid on two tickets to South America because I needed a holiday and I wanted to take my son to bond and create amazing memories. Six months later, my four-year-old son and I were off on a three-week trip through South America. We had the most amazing time travelling through Chile, Argentina, Iguazu Falls on the border of Paraquay and Brazil. We saw the main sights in each city and country we visited but now when we speak about the trip, my son only ever comments on three things:

1. A playground we went to in Buenos Aires. This was the only playground we went to on the whole trip (apart from some rusted swings on the way to visit volcanoes in Chile), and it was a highlight for him.

2. The beach. We live right near the beach in Melbourne, and he can go there anytime he likes.

3. Hot dogs. I rented an Airbnb in Rio De Janeiro, so we had a proper kitchen, instead of being in a hotel room. There was a market nearby and he tried a local hot dog. He was obsessed with them and asked me to make them every chance he got on that trip.

Giving your kids amazing lifestyle outcomes does not require you to spend tens of thousands of dollars or fly halfway across the world on big trips. Kids, particularly younger ones, will often get far more joy from you spending time with them and doing the simple things like going to the playground or the beach or eating a hot dog. If travel and holidays are a key lifestyle item for you, factor them into your plans, but don't lose sight of one of the key reasons to go on a holiday, which is to relax and connect with your family.

Summary

Balancing our short-term lifestyle desires with our long-term lifestyle security is one of the hardest things to get right. Having seemingly never-ending to-do lists and prioritising the lifestyles our kids or partners want makes it feel easier to go all in on short-term living, but being conscious of having an ongoing good lifestyle, rather than an excessive short-term lifestyle, is important. The last thing you want is to have to work longer or reduce your lifestyle later in life because you didn't give yourself future lifestyle security. If you don't strike a balance, you remove choices and options for yourself.

You need to be clear on whether you are spending money on something for a financial or lifestyle benefit. Don't allow your mind to convince you that something is not what it seems. Be clear on what your lifestyle expenditure is and allocate an appropriate amount, but not a disproportionate amount to it.

Sometimes great life experiences are on our doorstep, as my son taught me about the beach and the playground. Enjoy them, value them, appreciate them. They might be the convenient and low-cost lifestyle items that leave funds, time and energy available for other short- and long-term lifestyle successes.

PART FIVE
THE SELF METHOD – FINANCIAL

For a finance book, I have spent a lot of time talking about achieving your emotional and lifestyle goals. This is deliberate because that's what separates this finance book from others: the awareness that money alone will not create happiness and enjoying the different elements we want in our life is vital.

A big focus of mine is also to inspire you to make smart financial decisions, create better financial results and build wealth. If you want to become wealthy, no one is going to give it to you. While some people win the lottery or inherit a lot of money – you don't want to leave it to luck or put your financial freedom in the hands of someone else. You need to create your own wealth via smart strategies and investments, not just hoping for the best.

But why bother to improve our financial position or become wealthy? The most common reason and term I have heard people use over the years is 'financial freedom'. The ability to live and do what we want each day without a fear or focus on the financial considerations of those decisions. Work or not work, stay local or travel abroad, eat at home or eat out, buy the things we love, enjoy experiences and events. Just live with freedom and at ease with what we are doing each day.

Sounds nice, right? From the many clients I have helped to get to this position, I can guarantee you it is. They are content, happy, relaxed, calm and enjoying what they spend their time and money on. Let's look at how you can get there as quickly and easily as possible.

10
The GROWTH Financial Model

We all want to grow our finances (or at least I assume you do, or you wouldn't be reading this book). Whether we like it or not, money is a key part of our lives and is needed for many of the things we want. Sometimes having more money or getting better investments and financial results can feel challenging and elusive. Not everyone has training with money and is an expert, but this does not need to determine our financial outcomes.

Anyone can grow their wealth by following and repeating the right behaviours and actions. How much will depend on factors such as their age, level of income, financial position they are starting from, what fixed costs they can't avoid (eg kids to feed and raise) and so on. Regardless, everyone can grow and build wealth if they want to. I emphasise if you want to. Nothing can be achieved if you don't have a genuine desire to want to improve it. You need to be willing to put time and effort into better managing your finances, prioritising it, and seeing it as an actual goal of yours.

So just ask yourself, do I want to get better financial outcomes? Do I care about it? Am I willing to put ongoing time and effort into making it an important part of my life?

If you said yes, then great. The good news is making that commitment is easy, and once you have the systems and steps in place, maintaining it is easy too. It's a matter of building that and consistently repeating it month in month out. If you do that, you will see your wealth grow over time. The ultimate outcome of this will be financial freedom. Only you will know what financial freedom means to you and perhaps how much money you need to achieve it. You can do it, if you want it enough.

Let's grow your wealth

The financial model of the SELF Method is aptly named the GROWTH Model.

G – Goals

R – Returns

O – Opportunities

W – Wealth Accumulation

T – Time

H – Habits

The GROWTH Model is a great way to help you achieve your ultimate financial outcomes by focusing on the things that matter when it comes to growing wealth. It helps you focus on the key steps, behaviours and actions that will fast track an increase in your wealth and ensures it is sustainable and long term.

There is no point having a short-term surge of activity, followed by long periods of no effort, when trying to grow your wealth. It won't work and it is a waste of time. By following the GROWTH Model, you will get results and you will be well rewarded for the effort over time.

Goals

Just like you may have lifestyle goals such as the house, pool, private school or car, you also need to set financial goals. Management thinker Peter Drucker is quoted as saying, 'You can't manage what you can't measure'. What this means is you can't know whether you are successful unless success is defined and tracked. This is also true for your personal finances. You need a clear set of targets to aim for. What are yours? Write them down now. As always, include the item, the target timeframe and the amount.

Ask yourself the following:

- Is it a net wealth figure you wish to hit?

- Is it an investment portfolio worth a certain amount by a certain age so you could retire early and draw on that money until you can access your retirement savings?

- Is it a passive income stream of an annual amount by a certain age?

- Is it gifting a certain amount to your children at a future date or as an inheritance?

- Do you want to own your home or a certain number of properties, debt free, by a certain timeframe?

Write it down, and use a vision board for this like earlier if it will help.

In a study conducted by Prof Gail Matthews, a psychologist from the Dominican University of California, it was revealed that those who commit their goal setting to paper achieved more compared to those who were simply asked to think of what they wanted to accomplish in life.[10] It confirms that setting goals on paper makes them tangible and realistic.

In the same study by Matthews, it was revealed that accountability works wonders for increasing the achievability of your goals. A 40% improvement in fact. It doesn't necessarily mean that you need to have peer support, although that would help. You can hold yourself accountable by simply reviewing your documented goals and plotting your progress, so you are compelled to complete your actionable tasks and reach your goals.

Many of us may follow this advice or proven approach for setting goals in our life, but perhaps you haven't been or have not diligently done this with financial goals in particular. It's important to set specific financial goals, write them down and track your progress to ensure a higher chance of achieving them.

Returns

Several people could be credited with the quote, 'Sometimes the biggest risk is taking no risk at all'. Regardless of who said it, it is true when it comes to investing and growing wealth. I have seen people cost

---

10 Gardner, S, and Albee, D, 'Study focuses on strategies for achieving goals, resolutions' (Dominican University of California, 2015), https://scholar.dominican.edu/news-releases/266, accessed 18 May 2022

themselves millions of dollars because they sat and waited in zero-to-low risk and return land for years. In many cases a lack of action or an unwillingness to take on some level of investment-related risk can be the biggest determinant of the returns we receive on our money.

In recent years this has been particularly true because globally we have been living through some of the lowest interest rates in history. At the same time, central banks globally have been pumping more money into the economy and also stimulating it in other ways through government grants and tax cuts. While this depends on which country you are living in, it has been common in many nations globally. This means that despite the sharp falls in markets due to Covid-19 (for a short period of time) overall 'riskier' assets such as shares have significantly outperformed cash and bank savings returns. This has also been the case over the longer term. The following chart shows how this has occurred over time.

If you combine taking no risk on what you invest in, with how much you invest, then the gap in wealth accumulated is significant. For example, if you have not invested at all, then almost zero returns have been generated in cash. Compare that to investing regularly, plus perhaps magnifying that further with borrowed funds (where the cost to borrow has been so low) and the difference in wealth is staggering. As explained earlier, gearing (borrowing to invest) does come with

Returns (% per annum)

	1 Year	5 Years	10 Years	20 Years	30 Years
Australian shares	30.2	11.5	9.4	8.4	9.7
International Shares	27.5	14.7	14.8	5.1	8.3
U.S. Shares	29.1	17.5	19.0	6.5	10.8
Australian Bonds	-0.8	3.2	4.9	5.6	7.0
Australian Listed Property	33.2	5.8	11.8	6.9	8.6
Cash	0.1	1.3	2.2	3.8	4.6
CPI	3.8	1.8	1.8	2.4	2.4

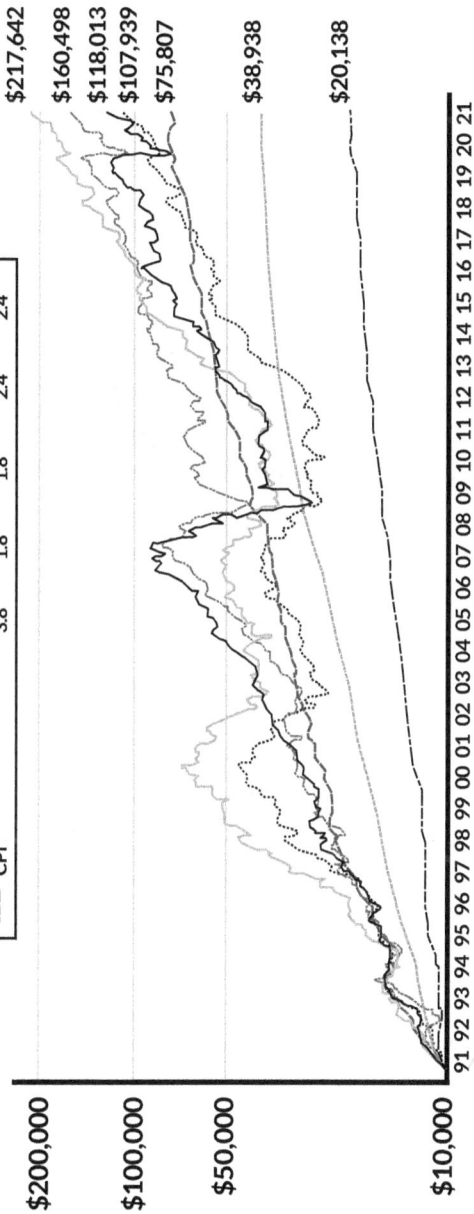

$217,642
$160,498
$118,013
$107,939
$75,807
$38,938
$20,138

$200,000
$100,000
$50,000
$10,000

91 92 93 94 95 96 97 98 99 00 01 02 03 04 05 06 07 08 09 10 11 12 13 14 15 16 17 18 19 20 21

Asset class performance, 1991–2021

Source: Vanguard

risk, but over long timeframes, with the right invest-ments selected, the old saying of the greater the risks, the greater the potential returns, will often prove to be correct. It's not for the faint-hearted, so it is vital that you find the level of risk that suits you, but taking no or minimal risk is likely to lead to lower investment returns and a slower growth of wealth.

As shown in the following figure, while investing in shares has its ups and downs and may feel volatile in short time spans, if you consider the chart from the perspective of the upwardly sloping line that goes from the bottom left to the top right, and medium-to long-term timeframes, it is a consistent upwards trend. You will see the various major events listed on the chart. When we are caught in that particu-lar period of time or major 'news' item, it's normal human psychology to think this is 'different', 'worse', 'bigger'. However as you can see, that event passes and the next event will eventually come along and be the next thing to worry about. But, never have they stopped that line from gradually going up and up. A focus on that line instead of the solid up and down area is what can allow you to stay calm and be a suc-cessful investor.

Opportunities

You need to put yourself in a position to take advan-tage of opportunities when they arise. It's hard to achieve this if you are reactive or chasing your tail.

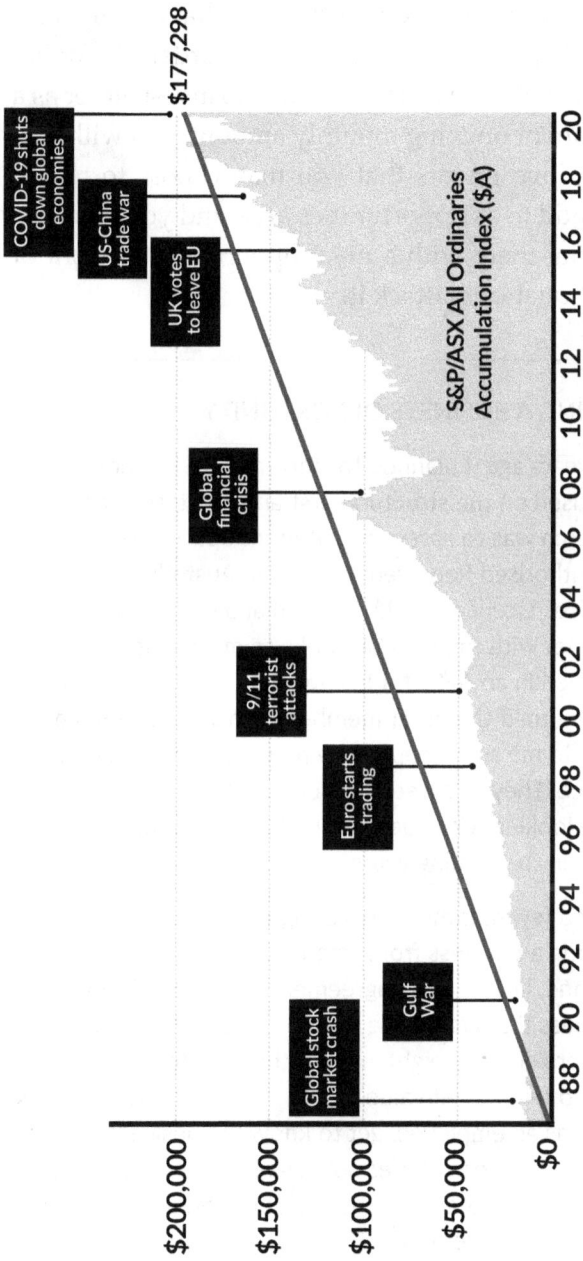

Growth of $10,00 over 30 years to December 2020

Source: Perpetual & FactSet

You instead need to be proactive and have your structure and financial management in order. By doing this, you will have funds available to invest either as a lump sum or ongoing monthly amount, you will hold existing investments that you may choose to reallocate or add to as opportunities arise and you won't be left sitting there with a great opportunity in front of you but unable to attack it.

SEIZING A BUSINESS OPPORTUNITY

Ten years ago, I planned to start my own business. I focused on the structural first and one task in my research was to assess my different options for being an Authorised Representative of an Australian Financial Services Licence (AFSL). I looked at a range of options and met with them. I also spoke to my dad as he was involved in an AFSL for his own business. I asked him to confirm if the other members of his AFSL would be open to me setting up a new practice and using their licence. They all agreed, but one of them also said they were looking for a succession plan as they wanted to retire in the coming years.

After a few months of exploring the pros and cons of starting a business from scratch versus buying into this one, I came to an agreement with the existing business that would see me purchase half the practice in approximately eighteen months' time for a pre-agreed fair market value. In the meantime, I would work there as an employee, get to know the business and its clients, and both parties could see if it was a good fit. After the eighteen months this all proceeded, and ten years have since past.

I was not planning to buy a business, I wanted to start one, but as I explored and researched my options, I could see a range of positives to buying into an existing practice. The main downside of buying into a medium-sized business was it came at a large cost, but after I weighed it up, I felt it was a wise investment. At the time I was only twenty-nine, but because I had been disciplined in investing for some time, I had a share portfolio and property assets with equity in them. I used the assets as part of the security to borrow for the business purchase.

If I had not put myself in that financial position earlier, I would not have been able to afford to buy the business and would not have been able to obtain the loan required to do so. I would have missed out on this excellent business and investment opportunity and my only option would have been to stay in my existing job as an employee or start a business from scratch. Preplanning and building up your position are key to scaling up and increasing your wealth as new opportunities present themselves.

Two big recent examples of this were the global financial crisis from 2007–2009 and the Covid-19 pandemic during its earlier days in 2020. In both cases, global share markets fell significantly, and, in some cases, the amount that certain companies or sectors of the market fell in value was not justified. Just as share markets can go up further than they should at times, they will often overshoot when they go down as well, particularly during significant events such as these.

Such events require you to have a focus on both the returns and opportunities components of the GROWTH Model, a willingness to take some risk on the basis that strong returns appear to be possible, and to be in a position where you have capital to deploy to participate in the opportunity. It also takes a fair bit of courage, guts and a contrarian view. During times like this, every piece of media and person you talk to will be negative: negative about the world, the economy and the share market. It's hard to think the opposite of that when that is all you are seeing or hearing.

Another challenging part about making sure we can benefit from opportunities is that it takes two forms of patience. The first is the patience to be employing the steps I outlined in the structural and wealth machine parts of this book. Such efforts are what will allow you to build your 'war chest' and have funds or equity available to deploy. The second form of patience required is to be willing to bide your time and wait for the best opportunities to arise. This is hard to do because unlike when bad events are occurring and the news is terrible, when things are going well, all the news and stories you hear are good. Your friends at the BBQ are talking about this property they bought, or how much of a bitcoin expert they are or how well the stock market is going. We too want to get in on the action. While often it is appropriate for you to do so, sometimes we need to recognise when an opportunity has either fully or significantly passed. This is when the froth and bubbles are starting to surface, and the likely upside is minimal. It's not easy trying to take the opposing view of others or to consistently show patience in our decision making, but you will be rewarded with great investment opportunities over time if you do.

SHARE INVESTMENT OPPORTUNITY

Covid-19 wiped huge amounts off share markets globally. It was a big fall in stock prices and it happened very quickly. As it was unfolding, I began assessing the market falls against prior market crashes. What I saw surprised me in the sense that it was one of the bigger falls that had ever occurred in such a short space of time.

I felt the reaction and reduction in company values was excessive and, as many stocks fell by 40% plus, I believed the potential downside risk was now quite low. On the flipside, I believed the potential upside, when the world progressed through and past the pandemic, was significant.

While I did not want to go back to the 'ugly debt' position I was in after my divorce, I was willing to borrow (good debt) to invest in quality companies that appeared to be grossly undervalued. So I did.

I took some risk. I focused on potential returns and the opportunity that was presenting and I was greedy when others were fearful. I invested at the exact bottom of the market. I am in no way saying I predicted the exact bottom, no one can do that, but it doesn't matter if it was perfect timing or just okay timing, the point is, I followed the important steps to investing successfully, went against the grain when there was

sufficient evidence to do so and was strongly rewarded
as markets shot up quickly in April 2020, continued
upwards and then burst up again in November 2020
when positive news about vaccinations started to filter
through to the world earlier than expected.

LIFESTYLE OPPORTUNITY

As my partner and I brought ourselves and our four
kids together as a family, a major step in this process
was moving in together. Initially we rented, but after
some time, I wanted to buy our home so that we felt
more settled and secure. I started looking around and
the property market in Melbourne at the time was
absolutely booming. I did not feel it was a smart time
to be buying property, and so it would not be a wise
financial decision. My partner wasn't in a rush to buy,
and we agreed taking our time was not going to create
any impacts on our emotional or lifestyle areas of the
SELF Method. Buying a home can be emotional, but it's
important to stay grounded and remember the right one
will come up at the right time. Once we got really clear
on the area we wanted to live we were ready to go, but
there was one downside: the property market was still
cracking hot. In my view. too hot.

With four kids, I knew we needed a home with a good
size yard and good internal space. I wanted the right
option for the long term. From prior property purchases
I had learnt that property value is in the land, so while
a home is predominantly a lifestyle decision, you still
want to make it as good a financial decision as possible.

Eventually I found a property in the perfect location. It
ticked all the emotional, lifestyle and financial boxes,

and we decided to buy. Enter Covid-19. Over the course of March 2020, Covid-19 went from this thing no one had heard about to taking over every news bulletin and leading to lockdowns of different parts of our lives. This included stopping residential property auctions, open for inspections and almost all real estate activity. As a result of this huge and sudden shift, the property was put up for private sale with a substantially lower asking price, and we started negotiating well below that to get ourselves the best price possible, knowing that even if others were interested, it was near on impossible for them to even view the property. Once again, a combination of putting ourselves in a position to be able fund the purchase and taking a patient and measured approach meant we achieved a successful outcome.

Just like I could never have predicted the bottom of the market, I also could not have predicted Covid-19 or the timing or impacts it inflicted on the property we purchased, but it is not about predicting the future. It is the pre-planned positioning of your finances and the willingness to be patient that are the key factors in successfully taking advantage of opportunities. If you get these two things right, eventually things will present themselves that make it obvious for you to pursue them and you have put yourself in the position to strike.

Wealth accumulation

We don't go from zero to millionaire overnight. It is an ongoing process of wealth accumulation. In the earlier stages, growing your wealth can feel extremely challenging. It is slow and hard work. But as you accumulate wealth, it will become easier. If you have not yet accumulated much wealth, remember that if you stick at it, it will get easier, not harder, to grow your wealth. If you have already accumulated a lot of wealth, this explanation will likely resonate with you.

The first million dollars of wealth will be by far the slowest and hardest million dollars you ever create. I am basing this off people who start with nothing and do not inherit a significant sum or win the lottery. You start at zero and work your way to one million, through a process like what I explained with the wealth wall. Why is this so hard?

The first eighteen years of your life are spent predominantly at school. You might get a job, but it will likely be low paying and not full time. Then you might go to university, get an apprenticeship or start working in your first full-time job. Your income is likely to be relatively low as you build up your qualifications, skills or experience. For most people, seeing significant increases in their income before around age twenty-five is unlikely. You may also be going through a phase where your parents provide less financial support, and you take on more responsibility for the costs of life. By around this age, many people are only starting to make strong inroads in their careers, earning capacity and ability to better manage their finances. If your career and income progress well and you do put in place some strong savings and investment structures, you should start to see your wealth grow, but it will usually still take many years to reach that first million dollars of net wealth.

However, once someone does get to $1 million of self-made wealth, it is likely this has happened via a combination of strong earnings capacity, good savings, investment discipline and a series of wise financial decisions. As a result, taking yourself from $1 million to $2 million and $2 million to $3 million and so on becomes easier, and the time between each million of increase in net wealth becomes shorter and shorter.

The reason this explanation and realisation is important is because it can be easy to give up on the concept of becoming wealthy. If that first $1 million feels hard and unobtainable, it's understandable that we would abandon our pursuit of wealth. If we instead have a mindset of wealth accumulation, we can better focus on the gradual increase and improvement of our position and see that we are progressing and heading in the right direction. Over time, this accumulation will gather pace and build on itself and the process of becoming wealthy becomes easier and faster.

Time

When it comes to investing and developing wealth, time is your best friend. The following figure illustrates the power of time. One dollar, yes just $1, invested in Australian shares in 1900, with earnings reinvested along the way, would in 2020 be worth a whopping $757,784. Over that time, Australian shares have returned an average of 11.8% per annum, Australian bonds 5.8% per annum and Australian cash 4.6% per annum. Without even adding to the $1, just by having the earnings from it reinvested, you can see the huge impact that time had on the value of that investment.

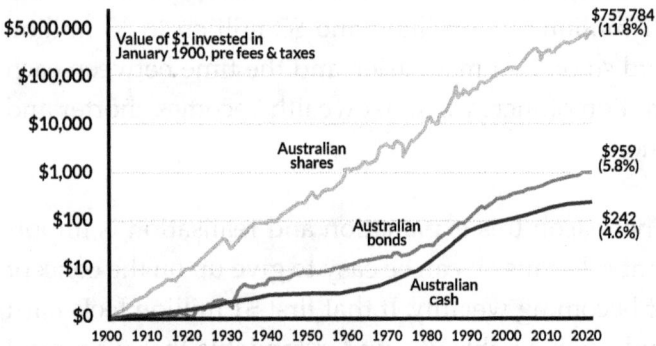

Shares versus bonds and cash over very long term – Australia
Source: Global Financial Data, AMP Capital

Time is a key part of the wealth accumulation process due to what Albert Einstein referred to as the eighth wonder of the world: compounding. Compounding is considered a wonder because you receive returns on your returns. Once you have a base of capital invested, as that generates both capital growth and income returns (interest or dividends) it is deriving those returns on a constantly increasing number. If you continue to reinvest these amounts, you will see this compounding affect grow and your money starts working harder for you. It starts to do a lot of the heavy lifting on your behalf and is another factor that makes the wealth accumulation process easier and easier.

The graph below shows the power of using compounding. Based on an initial investment of $10,000 in the S&P/ASX All Ordinaries Accumulation Index, held from 1990–2020, the investment would have grown to $91,256 without reinvesting the earnings (no compounding). This is compared to $177,298 if the earnings were reinvested. The result is almost doubled simply by capturing the power of compounding.

——— S&P ASX All Ordinaries Accumulation Index

——— S&P ASX All Ordinaries Price Index and non-reinvested dividends

Total returns: Dividends reinvested versus dividends not reinvested, December 1990 – December 2020

Source: Perpetual & FactSet

To maximise the impact of compounding there are three clear drivers:

1. The rate of return – the higher the better

2. The initial contribution – the bigger the better as it means there is more to compound on

3. Time – the longer the better

Many people do not harness this great compounding opportunity. Here are some of the most common reasons they miss out:

1. They are too conservative in their investment strategy and opt for lower-returning defensive assets like cash or bank deposits. This may avoid short-term volatility but won't build wealth over the long term.

2. They leave it too late to start investing or don't contribute much initially. This makes it more difficult to catch up in later life.

3. They attempt to 'beat' the market, by either trying to time market moves up or down or buying and selling particular stocks. Getting this right is easier said than done and investors often end up getting it wrong, buying at the top and selling at the bottom which destroys wealth.

4. They are not diversified enough.

5. Some people get sucked into investment opportunities that are too good to be true, which then fail. The key is to check the asset is producing fundamental value and not just dependent on the crowd pushing it higher.

Avoiding these mistakes and instead taking advantage of the power of compounding can put a huge tailwind behind your wealth accumulation. Like a yacht getting a sail full of wind, this can propel you along and give you a huge amount of assistance.

Habits

In the structural section of this book, I outlined a number of suggestions about how to set up your financial management structure. Getting this right from the outset is vital as there is no point adding effort and money into a poorly functioning system. Once you get your structure right, you need to keep it functioning well. If you can multiply time mentioned above, with a consistent, repeatable and process-driven approach to your money, then you will achieve far greater financial results.

They say it takes around 30 days to embed a habit. A big change to your money management habits can take longer than that and can be hard to stick to for the long term. Be clear with yourself that creating financial success is a long-term process and it requires you to develop and stick to habits for years. Breaking many years down into small brackets of time will make it easier. Think in weeks and months and keep it ticking over.

A great tool to help us is technology. Because our banking, savings and investing can be managed online, it's easy to set things up that force us to stick to our habits. Setting up direct debits to move funds for investment on a regular basis – that is your built-in habit right there. Commit to saving and investing a certain amount each month, click a button that forces the money to move to that place and keep it going each month. Don't change plans or course with your behaviours or habits, unless it's something that will enhance, not detract from your financial results.

Enjoying the fruits of financial success does not come over night and is not a one-off effort. It needs to be habitual and become part of your day-to-day life and maintained year to year.

Summary

You can make money hard, or you can make money easy. The GROWTH Model is an easy to remember and understand set of items. Follow the six parts of the GROWTH Model and financial freedom will be yours. To recap, the GROWTH Model is as easy as:

1. Set your financial **goals** as the target and motivation.

2. Recognise the importance of generating reasonable **returns**.

3. Set yourself up to take advantage of **opportunities**.

4. Stay on the path and keep going even if it feels hard sometimes. Remember, it's an ongoing process and about gradual **wealth accumulation**.

5. Use the power of **time** and compounding to support you and keep that supportive wind in your sails by continuously repeating the right **habits**.

11
Where To Invest

One of the biggest things I see people get wrong is not focusing enough on the items in the GROWTH Model. They spend too much time trying to pick the next big shiny thing they should invest in. Even people with no funds saved to invest talk about what they should invest in. This wastes a huge amount of one of our favourite financial allies – time. Getting the structures right and being in a good flow with the GROWTH Model is critical because that is what determines the ongoing allocation of funds to our investment portfolio. It is this contribution of funds that will create and make up the bulk of our wealth over time. Without this, where we invest has little impact because a huge return like 20% on a small amount of money is not much.

Once we have funds to invest and we are either consistently adding to that pool or we have built up our lifetime nest egg, what we invest in and where we put our money is vital. With a bigger asset base, compounding kicks in more and where we invest will determine what our returns are and how strongly that compounding will spur us along. The decision to either leave the money in the bank or venture out into other options that have historically provided better returns is a key to generating wealth.

It is also key to our enjoyment of managing our money. I would never suggest investing in something that is likely to generate a lower financial return just because you like it more. When investing for financial benefit (not lifestyle or family benefit) you need to take the emotion out of it. However, enjoying the process of managing our money and investments can of course make it easier to keep doing it wisely. There is no point investing in something you feel uncomfortable with in terms of the level of risk, the amount of management required or any stress or uneasiness it brings you. It also doesn't make sense to invest in things that don't fit your ethical and moral views.

What you invest in will likely have some elements of personal preference and bias for your own reasons. Over time and with different experiences, these preferences may change. Similarly, what you decide to invest in may change as you see different opportunities evolve with time. One investment is unlikely to be the best one throughout all market and economic cycles. Over your investment journey, the mix of what you own or buy will likely change.

With thousands of potential things you could invest in out there, it's understandable that it becomes confusing to work out what you should do. In the following section I'll share some helpful thoughts on some of the common broad investment areas where I find most people have questions, make comparisons and want answers on which one is best. History has shown that which investment performs best each year will often change on an annual basis. What's best for you may change, but the key thing is being invested over the long term to take advantage of the benefits of a well-diversified portfolio.

Property or shares?

I have invested in shares for over twenty-three years across large companies, small companies, local and overseas, traditional and contemporary industries and business models, directly and via group-based holdings such as managed funds, exchange traded funds and listed investment companies, and the list goes on. I have also researched and advised clients on such investments for over seventeen years.

In the direct residential property space, I have been involved for over fourteen years and owned multiple

properties. I have owned houses, townhouses, investment properties and Airbnbs in large cities and in
regional areas. I have also seen and discussed the hundreds (probably thousands) of properties that clients
have bought and sold over the years. To clarify, my
comments about property in this section are purely
in the context of residential property as that is where
most people's minds initially turn when they think
about property.

My exposure to both shares and property with both
my own money and advising clients has helped me
see the pros and cons for each of these options. Each
option's pros and cons may be more or less relevant to
you and your circumstances, and you may have reasons to prefer one over the other. That is 100% OK. The
purpose of this analysis is not to change your mind or
make you like one more than the other. It is to arm
you with more information to consider based on what
I have seen. From there you can use that information
to assist with your investment decisions.

If I had to choose just one investment out of property
and shares, which would it be? Shares. Don't get me
wrong, direct property can be a great investment and
can make you wealthy, and my experiences with property have overall been positive. But if am choosing
between property or shares, I have to go with shares.
Why? I believe shares have several benefits over property, which I have summarised in the following table.

Shares – Benefit	*Property – Opposing Negative*
You can start with very little, for example $100.	Direct properties have a significant upfront purchase price.
It has minimal or zero additional upfront investment costs. Many trading platforms are now essentially free, so you can put all your money to work in the actual investment at the start.	Property has a range of costs in addition to the high cost of the property itself. Depending on the country, this will involve initial costs such as government stamp duties, legal costs, transfer costs, other state or federal fees and charges. In Australia at the time of writing, stamp duty alone is approximately $50,000 – more than half the average annual salary – for the median home in Melbourne and Sydney. As it's percentage based it has also jumped by $23,900 over the past two decades in Adelaide and Canberra, increased by over $20,000 in Hobart and Darwin, and by over $13,000 in Perth and Brisbane.
It is simple and easy to get started.	Significant research and time is required to find the right property, plus significant time to save the deposit.
It is simple and easy to keep investing and growing the portfolio.	Each purchase takes significant time and money as per reasons above.

Continued

Shares – Benefit	Property – Opposing Negative
There are minimal ongoing costs.	Direct property has significant ongoing costs such as insurance, rates, maintenance, body corporate/strata fees, potential taxes and levies, agents' management fees and so on. This is usually many thousands of dollars per year.
You can easily diversify (not put all your eggs in one basket) and hold a range of companies and holdings.	Due to reasons stated, it can be hard to hold multiple properties and be diversified.
You don't have to borrow as it's a low-entry cost, but you can if you want to.	You will likely need to borrow due to the high cost.
Via shares, you can invest in property. This could be exposure to residential direct properties, commercial and industrial direct properties, as well as a whole range of properties listed in various stock exchanges globally. You could get part ownership of hundreds of residential properties, offices, factories, industrial buildings, warehouses, shopping centres and so on. You could be exposed to all these things starting with just a few hundred dollars.	Direct property gives you minimal options to diversify across property types due to the high cost of each property.
There are low exit cost fees.	There are high exit costs due to agents' fees, legal fees, government charges and the costs associated with presenting the property for sale.

Continued

Shares – Benefit	Property – Opposing Negative
It is easy to manage by viewing online anytime.	Hands-on management is required. Even if you have a managing agent it can be time-consuming, stressful and draining, particularly if you have a troublesome tenant or poorly built property.
Greater confidence of ongoing income via regular dividends or distributions.	There is the risk of periods of zero income if not tenanted.
It is more flexible if you need access to funds or want to change the portfolio. Simply sell a portion of your holdings.	Property is inflexible. For example, you can't sell a bedroom; you must sell the whole property if you need access to funds or want to change up your portfolio.
It is easier to manage and minimise tax implications both during the period of ownership and at the time of sale.	It is difficult to manage tax implications as it is one lumpy asset during time of ownership and at time of sale.
Valued daily so it's transparent and easy to know your ongoing returns and portfolio value at the click of a button.	It is only truly valued the day you buy it and the day you sell it.

Despite the list above, property can be a good investment. The main benefit it has over shares is it is more visible and tangible. People love the fact they can see it, touch it, look at photos of it, drive past it, show it to their friends and family. It's also an investment that people often talk about more openly.

But, property also has some myths or misunderstandings surrounding it. There is a mindset that property never goes down in value. Wrong. Many people say or believe you can't lose with property. Wrong. Also, while people understand the concept of rent on a property, they often don't understand the rent received on shares, generally called dividends or distributions. The following chart shows an example of the annual income paid by a particular stock (Telstra) via its dividends (rent), compared to cash.

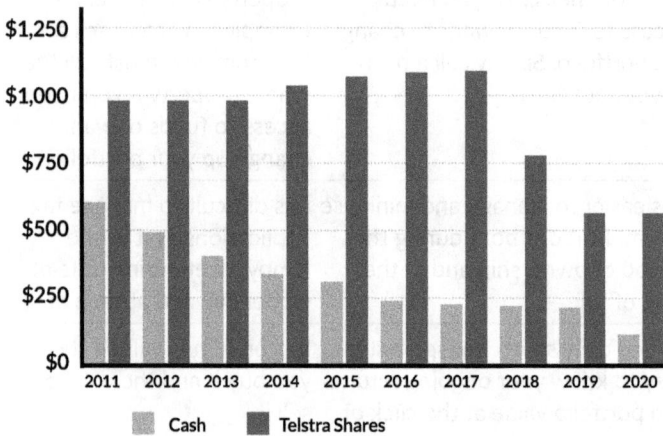

$10,000 invested in Telstra shares versus cash,
December 2010 – December 2020
Source: Perpetual & FactSet

Shares can provide excellent income returns, in many cases, higher than property on a percentage basis. This is known as the yield.

One recent study showed a diversified portfolio of shares and related holdings in Australian superannuation funds had significantly outperformed Australian house values.

A saver would have made a 157% cumulative return on their super over the past decade if they had invested in the median high-growth option, figures from super research house Chant West show. The median all growth fund return was even higher at 169%.

Australian house values rose 84.3% over the past decade, CoreLogic figures show, a little over half the return of high-growth super. Australian unit values managed just a third of super's return, at 50.4% in ten years.[11]

Whether property or shares are right for you will depend on your personal circumstances, the location and type of property, where both the share market and property markets sit at any given time in their cycles and what is happening across the economic cycle which could help or hinder either market.

11   Redman, E, 'Are you better off parking your savings in super or in property?', *The Sydney Morning Herald* (18 May, 2022), www.smh. com.au/property/news/are-you-better-off-parking-your-savings-in-super-or-in-property-20220517-p5am4p.html, accessed 22 June 2022

Blue chips or bitcoins?

Cryptocurrency and taking a punt on it has taken off like wildfire. A lot of people are involved and want to be involved and if someone has done well trading bitcoin or any other crypto, you are sure to hear about it from them. When prices take one of their regular nose dives, these same people go quiet.

In my view, buying bitcoin is not investing, it is speculating. It is highly risky and uncertain. The possible returns can be very high, but the inherent risks and the volatility of its value is also very high. The potential to lose everything is significant.

It is a market with minimal regulation, transparency and certainty, and as rules and regulations evolve, the risk that such changes could negatively impact the product and therefore those who have invested in it, is very high.

This was outlined in an article in the *Australian Financial Review* (AFR) on 18 November 2021.[12] The article explained that central banks were preparing to 'flex their regulatory muscle to take on the wild west where cryptocurrencies live'. Reserve Bank of Australia (RBA) head of payments Tony Richards warned that the 'value of many cryptocurrencies

---

12 Eyers, J, 'RBA warning on crypto fad', *The Australian Financial Review* (18 November 2021), www.afr.com/companies/financial-services/ central-bank-digital-cash-may-derail-crypto-s-run-rba-20211118-p59a2d, accessed 25 April 2022

could crash when central banks assert control over their monetary systems in a backlash against the sector'. This could mean for instance going after the massive energy consumption that goes into mining crypto, or tackling the issue of it being used as a preferred currency of organised crime and in the black economy. 'There are plausible scenarios where a range of factors could come together to significantly challenge the current fervour for cryptocurrencies,' Richards said in a speech. The AFR pointed out 'it was an uncharacteristically blunt warning from a central bank official about the potential response to the rise of largely unregulated private digital currencies'.

There are also central bank digital currencies and stablecoins that could impact crypto. They are digital money but with the added stability of official sanction. 'Central banks have been monitoring crypto since bitcoin's emergence early last decade as a decentralised means of exchanging value without oversight from banks,' writes senior reporter James Eyers. The official response is picking up speed. The Bank of England is considering a digital currency, the RBA is in discussions with other central banks, plus the National Australia Bank has openly supported a digital Australian dollar.

'Imposing control over a decentralised technology used by global online community that prides itself on challenging existing systems will not be easy, but crypto punters are on notice of potential crackdowns,' writes Eyers.

A couple of weeks after this article, $570 billion of market capitalisation was wiped off global crypto-currencies in one day and bitcoin was down 16% the same day.[13] This was caused by further global rumours about impending greater regulation, including from US authorities.

You will find plenty of people who are bullish about cryptocurrency, and they will provide a range of reasons as to why it will be a successful investment into the future. However it all plays out with crypto, the key thing to remember about putting your money into areas like this is that there is uncertainty. That can create significant volatility which is a risk and should be avoided where possible when investing. Some volatility and risk are required to generate higher returns than low-risk options such as holding money in a bank account, but it is important to be aware of when those risks may be too great or when the potential to lose your capital is high.

The risk of investing in blue chip high-quality global stocks and companies is much lower. The level of information available about the market and each underlying company is high. Humans can

13 Turner-Cohen, A, 'Crypto crash: $570 billion wiped off market cap after major sell-off over regulation fears' (news.com.au, 6 December 2021), www.news.com.au/c6adbadfbd3c2d57a176dded6062f0cb, accessed 18 May 2022

deceive investors with misinformation or unethical behaviours which can negatively impact a company and its performance – this risk is not completely avoidable but with the level of market oversight and disclosure and reporting requirements, this is far less common, particularly with medium- to large-sized companies.

While many people may think that shares are volatile, this is generally short term. As the following chart shows, over medium to longer timeframes the returns are consistently upwards and positive, as depicted by the line and explained earlier.

I suggest people stay clear of the hype and excitement of buying bitcoin or the next heavily publicised thing of a similar nature. It is speculating not investing and while it is possible to make a lot of money from it, the risk of losing everything is too great. Instead, buy quality companies and investments around the world, keep adding to your portfolio on a regular basis and let time and compounding do the rest of the heavy lifting.

What about a holiday home rental?

In the past, the idea of owning a holiday home was terrible from a financial perspective. All your capital tied up in something that hardly gets used, high ongoing costs of ownership, the headaches of having

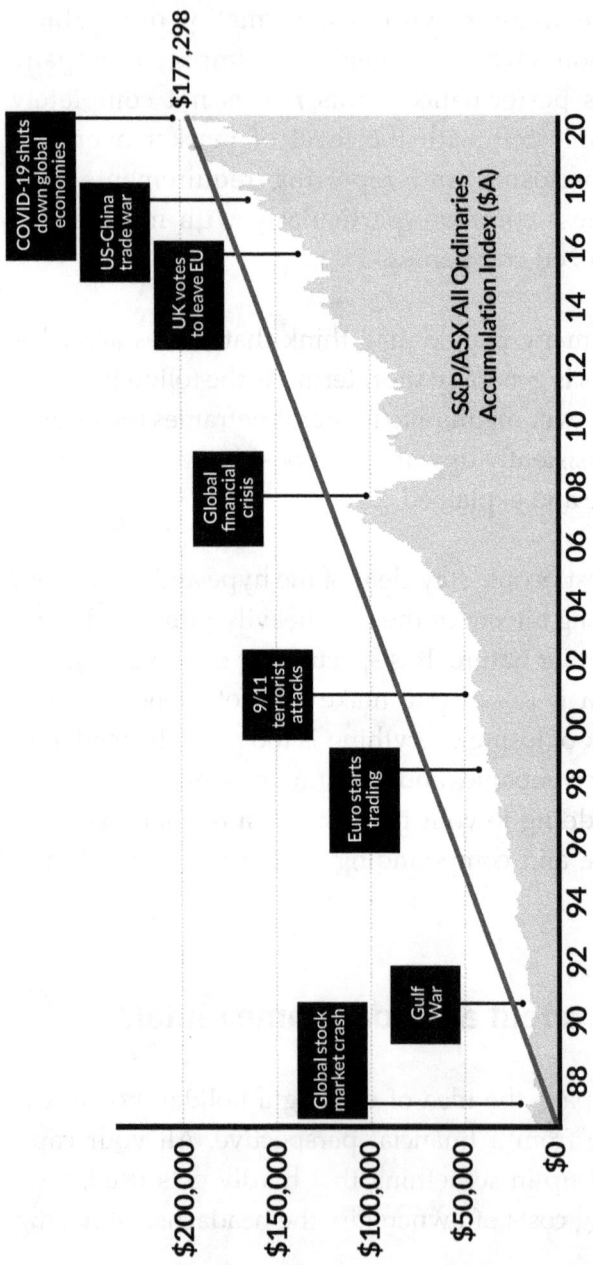

Growth of $10,000 over thirty years to December 2020

$200,000

$150,000

$100,000

$50,000

$0

88 90 92 94 96 98 00 02 04 06 08 10 12 14 16 18 20

$177,298

COVID-19 shuts down global economies

US-China trade war

UK votes to leave EU

Global financial crisis

9/11 terrorist attacks

Euro starts trading

Global stock market crash

Gulf War

S&P/ASX All Ordinaries Accumulation Index ($A)

Source: Perpetual & FactSet

to mow the lawn and fix things every time you go there instead of relaxing on holiday made it not worth the stress. In addition, usually no rental income was received on the property, and with the majority of holiday homes based out in regional or coastal areas, the capital growth rates were generally much lower than properties in capital cities. Financially, there was nothing to like, though it did tick many emotional and lifestyle goals.

My family was lucky that my grandparents bought a beach holiday house when my dad was young. Dad and his siblings spent huge amounts of time there, and when I was young, we would go there every summer. It was great to have this regular place to visit, so I know first-hand how such properties can add to emotional, lifestyle and family outcomes.

But this book is about balancing all the emotional, lifestyle and financial outcomes you want to achieve. With that in mind, a traditional holiday house is not something I see as a wise idea, unless you get to a level of financial security and wealth where you can afford to own such a property without it impacting your current or future financial freedom.

The good news is that since my grandparents bought their beach holiday house some sixty-plus years ago, the world has changed. One of the biggest changes is the introduction of systems and services such as Airbnb. The ability for property owners (homes or holiday homes) to generate a regular income through holiday guests has become a simple and common thing. This changes the potential financial outcomes of such a property because there is now the ability to generate rent and consider tax deductions on ownership and management costs. You may also see better capital growth in these areas as more people are visiting and taking an interest in the area. Covid-19 has also meant people are more able to work from anywhere, so the likely number of guests or potential future buyers has increased.

The other benefit is you can turn on or off the availability of the property. If you want to go for maximum income and financial benefits, always make it available. If you want to enjoy the place yourself, block the calendar and go for it. You can also do a mix of holiday letting and longer-term tenants. In the peak holiday seasons, take holiday guests where the nightly income is usually much higher, then in the quieter months, have a nice easy ongoing tenant. It is extremely flexible, and you can choose what suits you. It brings in a better balance across the emotional, lifestyle and financial than the traditional holiday house.

Having now managed my own holiday rental property for some time, I have learnt a lot and here are my key lessons to share if you are considering such a purchase:

- Guests have high expectations. Describe your property clearly and accurately. If it's nothing special or fancy, make sure the photos and description make that clear. If it is special and fancy, then make sure it lives up to expectations.

- It takes a lot of work. Don't think you throw it up on a website, guests turn up and you make a whole heap of money for no effort. It's not that simple. You must be realistic about what is involved with not just owning and managing any property, but managing one that has regularly changing guests. You can outsource the management, but this usually costs somewhere around 15% of your income, so you will first need to consider the financial benefit of owning the property.

- It costs a lot more to manage than a traditional property, even if you manage it yourself and don't pay the average 15% mentioned above. This cost will vary depending on how much of the work you do yourself, but in my case, I live a long way from the property so I need to pay cleaners, a gardener, a pool cleaner, laundry services and the usual costs of a property such as maintenance, insurance, rates, etc. You should also factor in your time required to manage the property. A different investment may not require so much of your time.

- Nightly income returns can be very good compared to a traditional long-term tenant, but you need to ensure your property is located in an area where there will be regular demand. There will be competition, so you need a property that attracts people to you instead of others. For example, my property has a pool and many others don't.

- Airbnb and similar websites can be a great source of marketing and bookings, but you should keep in mind that other marketing and admin is likely required to get maximum bookings. Also as these sites set their rules, sometimes you and your guests will not agree with their approach to things.

- To maximise the financial returns, you will need to rent it out in peak season. These short but high-priced periods such as Christmas, Easter and school holidays will likely generate approximately 80% of your annual income from the property. The old 80:20 Rule. This is also likely to be the time when you and your own family will want to use the property. So before purchasing such a property, be realistic and honest with yourself by asking, 'Am I really going to rent it out and make sure it generates an appropriate financial result?' Or are you going to use it yourself in peak periods? It's the old lifestyle asset versus financial asset honesty test.

- Capital growth compared to other investment opportunities (non-rental property or otherwise) will depend on where your property is located.

As capital growth can be a key factor in successful property investing, understand the potential for this (or not) with a holiday rental home.

- The flexibility is great: use it yourself, holiday let or permanent tenant – you choose.

- Its purpose might change for you over time. Initially it may be about financial returns, then over time as you are in a stronger financial position you might be able to focus more on using it yourself. This is also a positive and perhaps a good form of motivation to make it perform well, pay down any debt and enjoy it in the future.

- Some guests and the time and effort required to manage it can be a headache. There will be times when you find it a burden rather than a joy or benefit. Overall, though, most guests are good people and the technology to assist the host and guest is good.

So, what's the verdict, is a holiday home rental the way to go?

It comes down to the individual property and assessing its potential, but my general summary would be:

- If you plan to use it yourself in peak times, then financially it would struggle to stack up.

- If you rented it out for the large proportion of peak times, have a well-located property in a popular area and are willing to put the time and effort into managing and marketing the property, the financial outcomes from an income perspective can be good.

- Capital growth will be determined by the relevant economic and property market considerations in the relevant region, including demand and supply. Covid-19 certainly helped capital growth in many regional and coastal areas that would usually lag capital cities for capital growth returns. Whether this can continue is unknown.

- Given the time, effort and cost to manage a holiday home rental, as well as some level of uncertainty about the financial outcomes, from a pure investment and financial perspective, I wouldn't put owning a holiday home at the top of the investment list.

- From a balance perspective, factoring in emotional, lifestyle and financial benefits, a popular and well-managed holiday home rental is worth a look for those willing to take a more hands-on approach with their investments.

Summary

There are thousands of things we can invest in, and I have only covered a few broad examples. It is important to analyse each in detail and factor in your own circumstances, independent research and your tolerance for risk. You also need to factor in how much time and effort you want to put into managing your investments. For example, managing a share portfolio can be simple, while managing a holiday home rental can at times be a nightmare.

Overall, I find shares have a range of benefits over other options and can provide you with the ability to diversify across a range of asset types and locations. Focus on investing for the right timeframes and following the GROWTH Model to ensure strong long-term financial results.

12
Thoughts And Actions For Financial Success

Investing and growing wealth can be hard – hard on the mind, and hard on our thoughts. It often requires us to take the road we don't want to.

I've spoken about many key things that can make it challenging to create wealth. This includes:

- Patience

- Discipline

- Structure

- Balance

- Consistency of habits

- Not following the crowd

- Not allowing FOMO (fear of missing out) to take over your thoughts and actions

- Avoiding distractions

It's clear that becoming wealthy is not easy or simple. If it was, everyone would be wealthy. In order to have wealth, you need to spend time and energy thinking about it and prioritising it. You will not have wealth unless it is a deliberate part of your day-to-day thinking and actions. You also need to evolve your plan as things change over time.

To want to do this, it must be enjoyable and for many, finances are far from that. Don't worry, I have solutions in this chapter that will allow you to think about and act on becoming wealthy and to enjoy doing it.

You have to want wealth to have wealth

You have to want wealth to have wealth. It's fine not to want wealth, there is no requirement to, but it's unlikely you will achieve wealth (or at least not your maximum potential) unless you truly have a desire and mindset to want it. A willingness to display and manage some of the above listed items will prove your desire to want wealth.

The reason we want wealth will be different for each of us. For some they grew up with little so they want greater financial security. For others it's about giving themselves and their family the best life possible, and for a small percentage, they love money and having a lot of it. But the one thing that's true for anyone who obtains wealth is that it can mean financial freedom. This can mean lifestyle freedom. This can mean career and work freedom, or day-to-day freedom. You will have options and choices, and be able to put time and energy wherever you want it to go, knowing that financial impediments will not hold you back. From material and monetary wealth, comes numerous other forms of non-financial wealth.

So have a think, do you want wealth? Do you want all the other benefits wealth can bring you? You must want wealth to have wealth, and you must manage the psychological challenges that obtaining wealth will throw at you.

Earlier in the book I spoke about spenders versus savers. Which one you are was likely determined at a young age based on how you were brought up and what you were exposed to. As an adult you will have a certain psychological understanding of money that will have been informed by the things you saw and experienced growing up.

You will also lean a certain way in terms of risk-taking and the psychology associated with how you manage or invest money. This was likely developed at a young age too, but will also be impacted by your level of expe-rience, education and understanding of money and how certain investments work. Generally, with greater knowledge comes greater comfort and willingness to invest in something if we feel it is sound and wise.

This is important because our emotions and our thinking around money and investing can play a huge part in our financial outcomes. Studies have shown human behaviour can be hugely detrimental to investment outcomes. The following chart shows a study completed by Dalbar Inc (2014 edition), 'Quantitative Analysis of Investor Behaviour'. It shows the US stock market return between 1984–2013 was on average 11.1% per annum, while the average US equity fund investor return was 3.7% per annum on average. The US market returned 11.1%, but the average investor in that market only got 3.7%. The researchers called this lost return of 7.4% per annum, 'the investor behaviour penalty'.

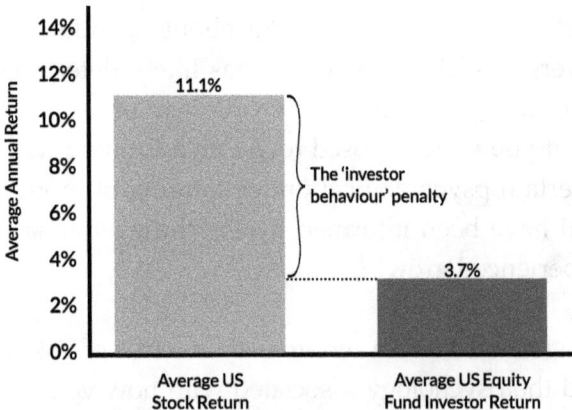

Average US stock market return versus average US equity fund investor return (1984–2013)

Source: Quantitative Analysis of Investor Behaviour by Dalbar, Inc
(2014 Edition)

As you can see, this behaviour has a huge impact on the returns received by the average investor and those lost investment returns would have a massive negative impact on their ongoing and long-term wealth position. In general this investor behaviour penalty is caused by us wanting to sell out of things when we should be buying, and wanting to buy things when we should be holding or selling. Being aware of your emotional and psychological state and finding ways to best manage this can be important to achieving optimal financial results.

Some tips for managing your emotions and psychology when investing are:

- Invest for the right timeframes. Typically, you should only invest in share-based investments if you plan to leave the funds invested for at least five to seven years.

- Only invest funds that can be used for that purpose and can be invested for the above timeframe. Don't invest funds if they are already earmarked for another purpose.

- Don't make rushed or rash decisions; remain calm and focus on the medium to long term.

- Diversify to reduce risk.

- Understand that things will go up and down, but as explained by the chart in the previous chapter, over the long term, it can be a positive upwards experience. It is time in the market, not timing the market. Don't try and get in and out regularly thinking that you can pick the perfect low and high points. You can't. No one can on a regular basis.

Control your mind, control your money

As our lives, careers and income levels evolve, this can present another challenge to us keeping in the right mindset about money. We see more money coming in, so we potentially start spending more and increasing our lifestyle by that amount. Maybe you think 'I'm doing well, I'm earning more, I'm kind of a big deal'. This is a financial mistake I like to call 'the income trap'. You fall into the trap of spending more and more as your income increases. This is understandable and again can be influenced by our psychological states, but it is not a good mindset from the perspective of achieving our financial goals. Allocate some of your increased income to lifestyle, but not all of it. Keep your structure in place and keep following the right habits. As you earn more, add more fuel to the wealth machine to keep propelling it towards the financial freedom and wealth you desire. Build that wealth wall faster.

As your wealth grows, it's also important not to think the wrong way about big amounts and small amounts of money. Remember the $500 per month that turned into nearly $3 million? That small $500 amount can create huge outcomes, so keep investing your available funds – even small additional amounts can become significant. While those amounts may start to feel smaller once you have a higher income and a higher level of wealth, they still play an important part in meeting your objectives and a key role in achieving your medium- to longer-term financial targets.

Many people never achieve high incomes, but they achieve great wealth because they respected the small amounts and stuck to the GROWTH process. One early client of mine had a relatively low income but had been saving and investing from a young age. By forty, the average annual returns from his investment portfolio were greater than his annual income from full-time work.

Keep your head straight, don't get ahead of yourself and don't let an increasing income send you off on to an excessive level of spending and lifestyle, especially not if it is on things that aren't increasing your happiness.

Similar thinking is required for big amounts. As you get to a higher level of financial success, reset your goals. Recognise that the amounts you used to see as big can now be seen as smaller. Set out a vision of bigger wealth goals and chase them. Once you have seen that $500 per month can turn into nearly $3 million, surely you must think $3 million isn't that much money? By that I mean, developing wealth of $3 million should feel achievable, but when you started reading this book or before seeing that example, $3 million probably seemed unattainable. Turn your mind to what you could achieve.

To assist with keeping your mind on track and controlling some of these thoughts, it's helpful to reconsider some of the earlier sections of this book about health. Our psychological states are related to health. As I like to say, healthy mind, healthy money. If we are in a good headspace by managing our physical and mental health, then we make better choices. Meditation can help with this a lot. It keeps us calm, energised, grounded and more able to make clearer and wiser decisions.

Gratitude is excellent for our mental health and financial decision making too. Gratitude involves writing down what you appreciate in your life, so you more clearly see what matters to you. For most people, this is not material items but family, friends, health and life experiences. When we see these are the keys to our happiness, we see spending money on material things as less important. As a result, we have greater funds available to invest to create the financial freedom we desire.

If you can control your mind, you can control your money.

Wealth parties

How we think and act about money plays a huge part in creating greater financial results. For many, controlling those thoughts and actions for a sustainable ongoing period can be challenging. Staying on course, making the wise decisions, ignoring the challenging thoughts, it's not easy.

Earlier in the book I spoke about the #makefinances-fun mindset. Now that you can see the psychological impediments of creating wealth, the importance of making finances fun should be clearer to you. If it's fun, you will want to do it more and you will get better results.

To bring all the elements discussed together, I recommend using wealth parties. A wealth party is a structured regular event for you to ensure you are reviewing and doing all the things that can enhance your financial success. Wealth parties are the way to create a positive and enjoyable way to review your finances, and if you are in a couple, talk about money in your relationship and life to ensure you do more than just read this book. You implement it.

So, how does it work? It's meant to look and feel like a party or a nice time out. Whatever that means to you, do it. There could be your favourite music, decorations or a theme, and your favourite food or your favourite drinks. Maybe you will get dressed up to feel and look great. Find your favourite part of the house to host the wealth party or go out to a favourite place. Do whatever brings a positive and enjoyable atmosphere.

While making it fun is vital, so you come back on a regular basis, it is still important to ensure you are dealing with everything you need to. You need a party plan which should include a list of items you need to review at each wealth party. You could add in non-financial things to the list as well. That way, as you go and tick a few things off at the party, you are rewarded with fun. It could be a break to put on your favourite song, mix a new drink, have a dance and anything that will make it into a nice night that just so happens to include your finances.

A potential party plan list could include the following (it will vary for single people and couples, but if you are single, get a friend involved and have fun with it together):

- How are we feeling about our Parental Balance Model? Are we in balance as individuals and as a couple, or are we overbalancing into certain areas and not paying enough attention to others?

- Is our structure working well? Is everything in order and up to date? Is our bank account structure in place and efficient through direct debits and automation and use of technology?

- How is our wealth machine running? Is it smooth or in need of a tune-up?

- How are we going with fuelling up our wealth machine?

- Have we got our boulders, rocks and pebbles on track, and are we filling up the container as full as possible?

- How is our wealth wall progressing? Are we adding bricks and building the wall as quickly as we want to?

- Are we meeting the 4Hs of the emotional model? Do we feel good, or do we need to make some changes to ensure greater harmony and happiness?

- How do the kids seem to be doing, and are money, time or energy required to assist them with any issues now or in the foreseeable future? How should we achieve this?

- Are there any burning lifestyle desires that we aren't meeting? Hobbies, holidays, home improvements?

- Are our longer-term lifestyle and financial goals on track? Are we balancing out the current, while also investing for the future?

By having regular wealth parties, you enjoy numerous benefits:

- You discuss areas that can sometimes be tense, boring or difficult in a fun and positive environment.

- Because you can make the wealth party look and feel however you want, you are in control of making sure it's fun. It doesn't need to be a chore or a negative event.

- By doing this regularly, I would suggest monthly, you are keeping on top of things so they never spiral out of control into a big mess or stress. Once you are in a good flow with the wealth parties, you will find they become efficient, and a lot of the time can be purely about having fun.

- Because you know any issues, concerns or important items will get discussed at these wealth parties on a regular basis, there is less need to bring up little issues on a week-to-week basis. Therefore, there is less likelihood of small arguments or tension around money as it's being handled in a positive environment, at a time and place that works for both of you and that has been set aside in advance for that purpose.

- You will have more structure, time and energy being directed to your finances and key life decisions, which means you will achieve better results.

Summary

Controlling your mind will play a key role in determining your financial results. You have to want it, and you have to work for it. You can't just enjoy the lifestyle and expect the financial outcomes to magically happen.

Keeping a strong and healthy mind will allow you to make better financial decisions. It will allow you to stay focused on what you are trying to achieve with your wealth and not be led off into the wrong areas by the psychological pressures that can come with achieving sustained financial success.

To make it easier, wealth parties will ease the pressure and stresses. They will ensure a regular touch point for reviewing your financial progress and allow you to celebrate the little wins along the way or get things back on track if they are veering off course. This will release some of the mental hurdles that can come with achieving financial freedom and allow you to keep going and feel good about what you are doing for your wealth creation and accumulation.

Our thoughts and actions are the key to reaching our financial dreams. Being aware of how they work and how to keep them in check will allow you to create the life you have always dreamed of.

Conclusion

Following the steps from this book will help to make you both rich and enriched. You can create the life and financial outcomes you desire. You can have what you want and ensure your partner and children enjoy the things they want. You can simultaneously enjoy financial freedom, life balance and family happiness.

The key to enjoying these amazing benefits is following the methodologies and models outlined. The SELF Method needs to be followed in order. You have learnt the importance of getting your structure right first as that is what gets you on track and keeps you there.

First, set your clear vision and believe you can live that life and level of financial success. Then cruise along in your efficient and well-oiled wealth machine to take you there via the fastest and smoothest route, avoiding bumps and dead ends.

Being open and communicative with yourself, your partner and family about what you want and how you feel about your life and money will allow you all to be on the same page. Together you will work towards and achieve your individual and family goals and dreams.

While structure and the wealth machine will set you on the right financial path, the lifestyle component of the SELF Method will make sure you have a great time along the way. A happy and comfortable home, fun family holidays and weekends away, continuing or restarting your hobbies and regular fun time outs via happy-hours. Enjoying a great lifestyle while using wealth parties will ensure you really can #makefinancesfun.

Using the GROWTH Model will make obtaining wealth and financial freedom much easier, as will understanding that your contributions will be rewarded and supported by time and compounding. It will take some effort, focus and control, but it is 100% achievable by anyone.

Keeping the Parental Balance Model visible to you will be hugely beneficial. Keep in mind that being a busy working parent is hard, and there are competing demands. Having a visual reminder of this model on your wall or fridge will help you continue striving for and striking the right balance across all areas of life. It will turn you into a skilled and adept juggling tightrope walker, capable of achieving amazing things including lifestyle and financial success.

As with anything, the key is doing it. Get started, take those first steps and create your destiny. You can do it. I know you can. I have faith and confidence in you. Follow what I've explained and put in the time and effort, and you will get what you desire and deserve. If you need some help, go to www.thefamilyfinanceguy.com.au and fill out our free financial and fulfillment scorecard to help guide your success.

Find me on Facebook, Instagram and Linkedin @thefamilyfinanceguy

I look forward to hearing of your success and hope that you can grab hold of the joy that comes from simultaneously achieving financial freedom, life balance and family happiness. Good luck!

Acknowledgements

Thanks to my dad for all his support of my career and work over many years. Thank you to Rod C, Lana and Nikki for your efforts in reviewing the book and providing valuable feedback. Thank you to Fiona and Neomal for introducing me to the amazing power of meditation. Thanks to the many family, friends and colleagues who have taken an interest in my book writing journey.

The Author

Josh Pennell started investing at fifteen and has invested in an array of successful global companies, properties and privately owned businesses. He also runs a successful beachside holiday rental in one of Australia's most popular coastal holiday destinations.

Josh holds a bachelor's degree in Economics and Finance from RMIT University and numerous post-graduate qualifications. He has been a wealth management and investment advisor for eighteen years and is a Director of Prosper Advisory Business & Wealth Advisors.

He is the expert finance commentator on radio station 94.1FM, and has featured in Smart Company, MSN Money and on some of Australia's most successful finance podcasts. Josh is also the founder of The Family Law Financial Journal and was a finalist in the 2021 Financial Planning Association of Australia Innovation in Advice Award.

Josh is a dad himself, so understands the combined demands of work and parental life. His personal experiences and his work advising hundreds of parents has given him deep expertise in guiding busy families to achieve lifestyle and financial success. Having created a happy blended family with four kids, Josh knows the most efficient ways for families to maximise their lifestyle and financial results. With a passion for both finance and family, Josh's purpose-built SELF Method and Parental Balance Model guide families to simultaneously enjoying financial and lifestyle freedom, life balance and family happiness.

You can connect with Josh and find useful tools, tips and insights at:

🌐 www.thefamilyfinanceguy.com.au

f @thefamilyfinanceguy

in @thefamilyfinanceguy

○ @thefamilyfinanceguy

www.ingramcontent.com/pod-product-compliance
Lightning Source LLC
Chambersburg PA
CBHW062056080426
42734CB00012B/2670